Pearson's Canal Companion

Stour Ring

WAYZGOOSE

Published by Wayzgoose
Tatenhill Common
Staffordshire DE13 9RS
email:enquiries@jmpearson.co.uk
www.jmpearson.co.uk

Eighth edition 2011
Updated 2014/2016
ISBN 978 0 9562777 2 5

Cobb's Engine House, Windmill End

"SO, Michael, can you tell us when you first became interested in canals?" I am a guest of the estimable Russell Newbery Engine Owners Club and forty or fifty eager faces are making eye-contact with me in a breezy marquee precariously attached to Titford Pumphouse, wondering if my inland waterways epiphany will resonate with theirs. Then, like Frank and Nancy, I go and blow it all by saying something stupid like: "Well, Andrew, I'm not sure if I have *ever* had an interest in canals!"

They are not on the same wavelength. No gasps, just audible silence. I am drowning in the toxic waters of 'The Crow'. But from deep in my subconscious, I dredge up the advice that successful public speakers focus on one face in the audience, so I latch on to a not unfriendly looking lady near the back and hear myself telling her that railways were my first love and that canals came along accidentally. She doesn't look entirely disinterested and, adjusting my lifebelt, I warm to my theme, informing her that I was working half-heartedly in the publicity department of an animal feeds firm when a job came up in the nearby offices of a monthly magazine called *Waterways World*. Having given what I thought was a reasonable impression of a canal enthusiast at the interview - why, I had even dressed the part - I was disappointed not to hear back from them. A fortnight passed and I screwed up the courage to telephone. "Oh yes, you got the job. Did no one tell you?" came the absentminded response. On such farcicalities, whole careers are forged, and I have been trying to escape from the canals for the best part of forty years: one foot on the accelerator, one foot on the brake. For as a means of making a living nothing could have been more conducive. And when Andrew asks me what my pastimes are away from the inland waterways, I find I cannot answer, because my work embraces them all.

An early assignment on the magazine saw me despatched to the Black Country. The canals were in a bit of a state (when aren't they!) and there were maintenance backlogs in abundance. Water levels were low, tunnels were closed, lock flights shut: doom and gloom abounded (when has it

Lock-wheeling

not!). Malcolm Braine at Norton Canes had been agitating for action and I was sent to interview him. Also, I had to call in at Keays boatyard, Walsall, and do a piece on a wooden tug they were building. In at the deep end on a snowbound day, but the seeds of a love affair were sown. At Pelsall I photographed a figure pushing a bicycle through the slush, bent over the handlebars in a manner reminiscent of an iconic picture in some northern coalfield by Bill Brandt. The first overbridge of the Cannock Extension stood starkly up against the snow like a portal to an underworld, and in the distance a misty line of poplars added sombre verticality to the whitewashed increments of horizontal wasteland. There was no way back, the BCN was in my blood; though a decade elapsed before I got to write a guidebook to it, and by then much of its character was haemorrhaging away. A paramedic at a road crash, I did what I could, and tried to convey what we were all too late to see. And I have been trying ever since, though it is increasingly difficult to find any indication of a pulse these days. But I trust I have yet to reach the day when the past becomes entirely preferable to the present, let alone the future. When it comes I will hang up my windlass. A guidebook compiler can afford to be wistful, but never disconsolate.

Towards the end of the entertainment (I use the term loosely) questions were taken from the audience, and that hoary old chestnut - "Do you have a favourite canal?" - raised its head. Happily, I had no difficulty in persuading them of my promiscuity in such matters: My favourite canal is the one I'm working on at any given time. The sporting equivalent of taking each fixture as it comes.

The lady at the back was stifling a yawn. None of us could help noticing that the bar had opened. Andrew was asking for a round of applause. It duly arrived; at the politer end of the scale than the ecstatic. Had there been a clap-o-meter present, the decibel level would probably have equated to that I received on Speech Day 1970, mounting the stage at Clifton Cinema to accept the Divinity Prize.

The Twenty-One
4

Stourport
Ring

Austcliff

R. SEVERN, STAFFS & WORCS CANAL Stourport 4mls/6lks/3hrs

FOR all practical purposes, Stourport marks the head of navigation on the Severn, and it is here that the through traveller by water exchanges the fluctuating currents of the river for the stolid waters of the Staffordshire & Worcestershire Canal.

Stourport itself suffers from a personality disorder: half convinced that it's a seaside town; half a rich heritage of canal wharves. But whether you have come here for a ninety-nine and a knees-up, or to pay more serious homage to Brindley's basins, Stourport rarely disappoints. To moor in the Upper Basin, listening to time being measured by the quarter beats of the clocktower's sonorous bell, is one of the inland waterways' most magical experiences. And whatever entrance the boater makes - locking up from the Severn under the benign gaze of the Tontine Hotel, or descending into the dripping depths of York Street Lock from the canal - there will be few steerers able to resist exploration of the basins, shunting back and forth like some busy tug; turning in wide arcs or honing their reversing skills. The original and largest - known as the Upper Basin - opened in 1771, and connects through two wide-beam 'barge' locks with the river. These impressive (at least in narrowboater's eyes) chambers were built sturdily enough to withstand the Severn's perennial propensity for flooding, and capacious enough for the indigenous Severn Trows. Between the barge locks lies the smallest

basin, thought to have been used as an assembly point and not as a wharf as such. A second link to the river, consisting of four narrow-beam locks in pairs of staircases, was opened in 1781. Here again the locks are separated by a small basin from which a drydock extends. Manoeuvring a lengthy boat between the staircase pairs can be tricky, and it doesn't help one's sang-froid that there is often a sizeable crowd of onlookers. At the top of the narrow locks, and contemporary with their construction, lies the Clock Basin, interconnected with the Upper Basin. On a peninsula between these upper, boat-filled expanses of water stands the glorious Clock Warehouse, headquarters these days of the Stourport Yacht Club whose comparatively huge vessels migrate up-river to winter in the security of the basins.

Once there were two basins which lay to the east of Mart Lane. Known expediently as the 'Furthermost Basins', they dated

Map labels

Head of Navigation
Gladder Brook
sewage works
70'
Areley Kings
Stourport on Severn
Basin Locks 29ft 0ins
Town Centre
5A 6 5 4
Stourport (csd 1970)
Lidl
7cemy
Stourport Swifts FC
WORCS CANAL
STAFFS &
9
Wilden Pool
R. Stour
Wilden
10 10A
54
45
8
site of power station
R. Severn
Severn Way
rowing
STOURPORT RING
Hartlebury Common
A4025
B4193
Redstone Rock
Stourport Marina
weir !
Lincomb Lock
7ft 4ins
Tel: 01299 822887
19

Bridge Names

4 Wallfield	8 Upper Mitton
5 Lower Mitton	9 Bullock Lane
5A Baldwin's	10 Oldington
6 Gilgal	10A Pratt's Wharf
7 Mitton Chapel	

from the early 19th century. The lower, reached through a wide lock, had a brief existence, closing in 1866 when the town gas works took over the site. The other basin flourished in an Indian Summer of commercial activity between 1926 and 1949 when coal boats for the power station discharged in it; their dusty black cargoes of Cannock coalfield slack being unloaded by electric grab and carried in hoppers along an aerial ropeway to the power station's furnaces. Subsequently it was infilled and a timber yard occupied its site, but it has been re-excavated as a major focal point of the regeneration scheme.

Another important element of the redevelopment of Stourport Basins concerns the return to life of the Tontine Hotel, refurbished for use as housing. It derived its unusual name from a system of speculative life insurance, the last surviving member of its original group of investors gaining full ownership of the building: fuel for skulduggery one imagines and the possibility of a plot which would inspire most detective story writers. In its heyday it boasted a hundred bedrooms, a ballroom and formal gardens spilling down to the riverbank.

The River

The Severn's official head of navigation is just upstream of Stourport Bridge where the Gladder Brook enters from the west bank, though occasional convoys of shallow-draughted die-hards do journey upstream to Bewdley campaigning to restore navigation to the Upper Severn. One waterway project which did not materialise was for a canal from Stourport to Leominster. A token sod was dug opposite the basins in 1797, but the ludicrously ambitious through route never came to fruition. No trace remains of Stourport's grandiose riverside power station, opened with a flourish by Stanley Baldwin in 1926. Pending any progress with the Upper Severn scheme, Lincomb Lock is the highest on the Severn. It

lies in a picturesque setting dominated by one of the sheer red sandstone cliffs which characterise the river in this part of the world. There is another such dramatic outcrop between Lincomb and Stourport known as Redstone Rock, a refuge, apparently, of outlaws in Cromwell's time. Opposite the rock, a well piled wharf marks the destination of the Severn's last commercial traffics above Worcester in the 1960s.

The Canal

Secretive, might be the best way to describe the Staffordshire & Worcestershire Canal's departure from (and approach to) its southern terminus at Stourport. Though sharing a wide enough valley with the Stour, the canal tends to be masked by trees and vegetation, and as a consequence has something of a reclusive character to it. Boaters not inclined to proceed beyond the confines of the canal are advised to moor above York Street Lock where visitor moorings are provided opposite the site of the canal company's workshops, redeveloped into not unattractive modern housing.

Leaving Stourport - as if by the back door - the canal is soon curving beneath the old railway bridge which carried the Severn Valley Railway between Hartlebury and Bewdley. There used to be a canal/rail interchange dock at this point. Rusty mooring rings set into a high brick retaining wall recall busier times. Another distant echo of bygone trading days is encountered by Bridge 10A, through which a branch canal long ago led down by way of a lock into the River Stour for boats to reach Wilden Ironworks across the valley.

 The 'narrow boat' route through the basins at Stourport - from river to canal and vice versa - involves negotiating two staircase locks which are unusual in that there is no need to ensure that the lower chamber is empty when going down.

Stourport

Map 1

Water on the brain has left Stourport under the illusion that it's a coastal resort. All the trappings are here: funfairs and fish & chips, steamer trips, paddling pools and amusement arcades. Day trippers pour in from the West Midlands to let their hair down and make believe they are really in Rhyl or Barmouth. Marginally more in touch with reality, us boaters can swagger about the town pretending that we've just come up with a cargo of oil from Avonmouth.

Eating & Drinking

BIRD IN HAND - Holly Road (between bridges 7 & 8). Tel: 01299 871515. Canalside. Open from noon. Food and Hobsons (of Cleobury Mortimer) beers. DY13 9BA

BLACK STAR - Mitton Street (Bridge 5). Tel: 01299 488838. *Good Beer Guide* listed pub overlooking canal offering food and Wye Valley Ales. DY13 8YP

BLOSSOM'S - York Street. Tel: 01299 829442. Quaint canalside tea room. DY13 9EE

THE HOLLYBUSH - Mitton Street. Tel: 01299 827435. *GBG* listed Black Country Ales and food. DY13 9AA

NAMASTE - Lichfield Street. Tel: 01299 877448. Indian restaurant adjacent Bridge 4. DY13 9EU

RISING SUN - Lombard Street (canalside Bridge 5A). Tel: 01299 822530. Little Banks's backstreet local offering good value meals. DY13 8DU

THE WINDLASS - Stourport Basins. Tel: 01299 871742. Cafe/restaurant housed in former canal workshop and stable. Open daily plus evenings Thur-Sat. DY13 9EW

Shopping

Co-op (with post office), Tesco Metro and Lidl supermarkets are most easily accessed from either side of Bridge 5A. On High Street look out for the mouth-watering premises of The Pie Creator. Across the street Gough's is a butcher/greengrocer featuring gluten-free pies. Two launderettes on Lombard Street.

Connections

BUSES - Diamond 3 & X3 link Stourport with Kidderminster every 10 mins Mon-Sat and approx. hourly Sun. Diamond services 294/5 run bi-hourly Mon-Sat to/from Worcester. Tel: 0871 200 2233.

TAXIS - Pardoe's. Tel: 01299 824924.

Kidderminster

Map 2

Famous for its carpets, its steam railway and for the occasional cup exploits of its football team, 'The Harriers', Kidderminster is a working town of considerable - if occasionally elusive - character. A bloated ring road divorces the canal from the town centre, but in the pedestrianised streets the roar of traffic soon dies down, and you can admire 'Kidder's' handsome sandstone and redbrick buildings; the way the River Stour plays hide and seek through it, and the statue of Rowland Hill. It certainly has Pearson's stamp of approval.

Eating & Drinking

LOVE FOOD ITALIA - New Road. Tel: 01562 60610. Delightful deli/diner open from 9am-3pm, Mon-Sat for breakfast/lunch and 6-9pm for dinner. Sunday lunch 10am-4pm. Nice items for the larder too! DY10 1AF

LA BRASSERIE - Mill Street. Tel: 01562 744976. French restaurant adjacent Weaver's Wharf visitor moorings. A plaque on the former dance hall next door recalls appearances by such illustrious acts as T. Rex, Fleetwood Mac and Captain Beefheart. DY11 6UU

THE WATERMILL - Park Lane, Bridge 13. Tel: 01562 66713. Canalside, all-day Marston's pub/restaurant housed in mock watermill. Limited off-side customer moorings. DY11 6TL

WEAVERS - Park Lane (Bridge 15). Tel: 01562 742717. Quaint canalside pub. Bewdley Ales. DY11 6TG

McDonald's, Frankie & Benny and Pizza Hut all canalside at Weavers Wharf.

Shopping

The shopping centre is comprehensive, lively and traffic free and has been boosted by the advent of the Weavers Wharf retail development which features a branch of Debenhams housed in Brintons former carpet mill. Look out for the bell which used to be rung in event of fire. There's a retail market on Thursdays and Saturdays. Launderette on Comberton Hill near Severn Valley Railway station.

Things to Do

SEVERN VALLEY RAILWAY - 01562 757900. One of Britain's premier preserved railways, the SVR runs up the valley via Bewdley to the Shropshire market town of Bridgnorth, a delightful ride in its own right, never mind the fun of being hauled by steam. Services run throughout the summer and on most other weekends and holiday periods. DY10 1QX

MUSEUM OF CARPET - Green Street. Tel: 01562 69028. Open Tue-Sat 10.30am-4.30pm, Sun 12pm-4.30pm. Admission charge. Exhibitions and demonstrations of Kidderminster's stock-in-trade. Souvenir shop. Entrance via Morrison's. DY10 1AZ

Connections

BUSES - Diamond services 3 & X3 link Kidderminster with Stourport at 10 minute intervals Mon-Sat, hourly Sun. Tel: 0871 200 2233.

TRAINS - frequent local services to/from Birmingham Snow Hill and Worcester etc. Tel: 03457 484950.

Taxis - Central Taxis. Tel: 01562 825522.

Wolverley

Map 2

THE LOCK INN - canalside Bridge 20. Tel: 01562 850581. Pretty canalside pub which also operates Old Smithy tea room (featuring Marshfield Farm ice cream) on the far side of the lock. Take-aways. DY10 3RN

Wolverley village, 5 minutes stroll west, offers another pub and some picturesque buildings and a Georgian church.

THE carpet-making town of Kidderminster has had its waterfront regenerated in recent years - all the usual suspects: fast-food outlets, supermarkets, ring roads and retail parks. Yet one or two of the old carpet factories remain intact, putting up with, if not exactly relishing, new 21st century uses as parodies of American restaurants and Designer Outlets.

South of the town two isolated locks, couched in the shadow of sandstone outcrops and bereft now of the lock-keepers' cottages which long ago accompanied them, are separated by a high, seven-arch brick viaduct over which steam trains of the Severn Valley Railway puff and pant their way between Kidderminster and Bridgnorth.

Passing through the centre of town, the canal used to penetrate a deep canyon of factory premises, but these have been demolished, along with another carpet works which once stood above Kidderminster Lock. Now two supermarkets vie for boating custom and provide good moorings in the process, but personally we still prefer (during daytime at least) those at the old town wharf (on the offside above the lock) which are overlooked by the splendid parish church of St Mary's (the largest in Worcestershire) and a statue of Richard Baxter, the 17th century preacher, teacher and pastor who wrote the hymn *The Saints Everlasting Rest*. New housing is spreading out north of Kidderminster, but the canal quickly establishes its more obvious rural charms. Wolverley Court Lock lies in a seemingly remote parcel of scrubland in an area once extensively used for sand extraction. Wolverley Lock is overlooked by a quaint pub, with a canalside patio which has the potential of transforming your lock routine into street theatre. North of here, delving into glades of balsam and convolvulus, bluebells and foxgloves, the canal is at its most beguilingly attractive.

The Elan Valley water pipe-line used to cross the canal between bridges 21 and 22, now it is culverted beneath it. Completed in 1907, this 73 mile pipe brings water from reservoirs in the Rhayader Mountains of Wales to the bathtubs of the Black Country. The pipe-line's construction at the turn of the century was a huge undertaking, and one of the last great adventures of the 'navvies': "rough, violent men, whose speech had foreign inflections and whose corduroys were caked with the mud of four counties," wrote Francis Brett Young in the preface to one of his most enjoyable novels, *House Under the Water* which was inspired by the project.

⚠ Handcuff keys required at Falling Sands, Caldwall and Kidderminster locks

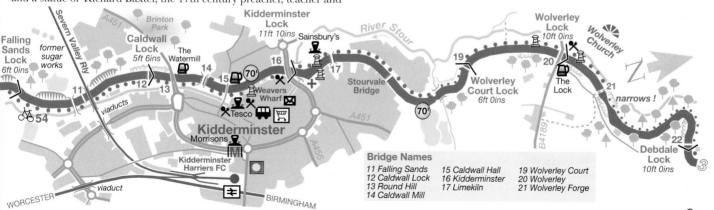

Bridge Names

11 Falling Sands	15 Caldwall Hall	19 Wolverley Court
12 Caldwall Lock	16 Kidderminster	20 Wolverley
13 Round Hill	17 Limekiln	21 Wolverley Forge
14 Caldwall Mill		

IS there a prettier, more demure length of canal in the country? Rivals spring to mind, but none lovelier than the Staffs & Worcs, winding its wooded way from Cookley to Stourton past Kinver with its church perched high on Kinver Edge. There is a "Toytown" ambience about this whole canal which the Swiss would thoroughly approve of. Arguably the prettiest length of all lies between Hyde Lock and Dunsley's diminutive tunnel. Here, bordered by woods on one side, the canal glides past meadows backed by a conifer plantation. It would be difficult to imagine a more rural scene, yet a huge ironworks stood in the vicinity for two centuries. In its heyday twenty puddling furnaces produced wrought iron and the premises lined the canal for some distance. But only the manager's house remains, and nowadays butter wouldn't melt in its mouth, innocent in its setting beside the towpath above Hyde Lock. Less innocent is the discovery that underground chambers were hewn out of the area's soft sandstone for the manufacture and storage of munitions during the Second World War. And even more

unnervingly, that these subterannean labyrinths were earmarked as a seat of regional government in the event of a nuclear war.

Barely had the ironworks' pandemonium ceased, when a new interloper arrived on the Stour Valley scene, in the shape of a curious little narrow gauge railway operated with electric trams. The Kinver Light Railway opened in 1901 and lasted only twenty-nine years, but in its short existence brought thousands of day-trippers from the Black Country to Kinver, flaunted by the operating company as the "Switzerland of the Midlands". On Whit Monday, 1905, nearly seventeen thousand passengers were carried along the five mile line from Amblecote, near Stourbridge. The 3ft 6ins gauge track (along which through cars ran from as far

The towpath is in pretty good condition for a rural canal, and used by walkers and cyclists alike. Short walks abound in the vicinity of Kinver where good car parking is available or you can use the bus from Stourbridge and walk back via Stourton Junction.

for details of facilities at Cookley and Kinver turn to page 13

as Birmingham) crossed the canal at Stewponey, ran alongside it at Hyde, and terminated at Mill Lane, Kinver where the pumping station now stands.

Stewponey was a focal point for boat traffic on the Staffs & Worcs. Facilities included a wharf, stables, toll office, workshop and employees' cottages. Even after the Second World War, in excess of fifty boat loads of Cannock Chase and Baggeridge Colliery coal was being worked through here to Stourport Power Station each week. But in 1949 the National Coal Board announced a florin surcharge on each ton of coal loaded on to boats. Not entirely surprisingly, the traffic rapidly transferred to rail. A few years of desultory day boat trading to Swindon Steel works, 'railway' boats off the Stourbridge Canal, and occasional cargoes of baled wool to Stourport from 'up north' followed, and then, without anyone really noticing, the working boats were gone.

Stewponey doesn't find its way on to Ordnance Survey maps, but is a name of local currency, thought to be derived from an old soldier, returning with a Spanish wife from the town of Estepona, who opened an inn here, the name of which was soon corrupted by Black Country vowels. The inn was rebuilt as a roadhouse in the Thirties, one of those huge joints which were honeypots in the early days of motoring; there was even a Lido in the grounds. One feels short-changed that it has been demolished and replaced by housing completely devoid of any aesthetic ambition. Imagine for a moment that the Lido was still in use, and that

Dunsley Tunnel

you could still reach it in the jolly company of one of the Kinver Light Railway's trams, and then calculate just how much Progress has defaulted on the Past.

At Stourton Junction four chambers raise the Stourbridge Canal up on its way to the Black Country. Canal junctions don't come much more

Cookley Tunnel

attractive than this and, even if your itinerary commits you to the Staffs & Worcs, you could do worse than spend a night in Stourbridge, little more than an hour and a half away as described on Map 33.

North of Stourton Junction, the canal - known colloquially as the 'Stour Cut' - bridges the river of the same name. The setting is idyllic, the river tumbling over a shallow weir just upstream of the double-arch aqueduct, and issuing from the adjoining bend, a broad pool. Close by, a peculiar cave is cut out of the rocks at water level. Known as "Devil's Den", it is thought to have been used as a boathouse by the Foley family of Prestwood Hall.

Southwards from Stewponey, the river is the canal's constant companion, the man made waterway keeping pace with the Stour's gradual descent to the Severn by way of occasional, isolated locks of great charm. It is difficult to think of another canal bounded by so many trees, their presence broken only by occasional outcrops of Triassic rock. The most dramatic of these - a real cliffhanger if ever there was one! - is near Caunsall where the Bunter pebble beds of Austcliff Rock loom over a bend in the canal. Little less spectacular is the canal's burrowing beneath the old iron-making village of Cookley, its houses seemingly precariously poised over the northern portal of Cookley Tunnel.

4 STAFFS & WORCS CANAL Greensforge & Swindon 4mls/8lks/3hrs

T HE countryside empties. Wales is only the width of an Ordnance Survey map away. These are the landscapes of Francis Brett Young, and no-one has ever written better about the area between the Black Country and the Welsh Marches. Try and get hold of a copy of *Far Forest* or *Dr Bradley Remembers*; either would make admirable reading before 'lights out' on your cruise.

Smestow Brook, a tributary of the Stour, is now the canal's chief confidant and friend. In the woods below Gothersley Lock stood a canal company roundhouse, a twin to that at Gailey (Map 31) now restored and used as a canalside shop. Both roundhouses date from the year of Trafalgar. The Gothersley one marks the site of an important canal wharf provided to serve a sizeable ironworks which existed here until the 1880s. The roundhouse itself, a gaunt ruin for many years, was storm damaged in 1991 and its base is now the focal point of a picnic site and visitor moorings. The ironworks has vanished as well, its forges, furnaces, tramways and wharves superseded by ivy, ash, balsam and butterbur.

Greensforge is a delightful mooring place. Its name recalls the existence of another vanished forge, one which became a mill, the big, four square building which remains intact and glimpsed through the alders and willows lining the Smestow. Stroll down the lane and you'll discover its macey, long dry mill pond, an obvious declivity in the reed beds. Nearby an arm extends into Ashwood Basin, now a marina but once an important interchange basin with the Kingswinford Railway, a colliery line dating from 1829 whose first locomotive, *Agenoria*, is now in the National Railway Museum's collection in York.

The lovely garden which borders the canal south of Bridge 36 belongs to John Massey, owner of the adjoining Ashwood Nurseries, recipients of a Gold Medal at the Chelsea Flower Show of 2016 for their Hepaticas. The garden is private, though open to the public on selected dates. The nurseries are best accessed from Greensforge Lock.

Between Greensforge and Hinksford locks the canal is bordered by the contrasting images of woodland and a huge static caravan park. Hinksford Pumping Station is one of several waterworks in this part of the valley. Yet another ironworks lined the canal at Swindon. This one survived until as recently as 1976 and specialised in rolling silicon steel sheets for the electrical engineering industry. Not that you would credit it now, the site being covered by the neat lawns, barbecues and conservatory extensions of modern housing. The works was owned at one time by the Baldwin family, of which Stanley became Prime Minister. Note how the towpath briefly changes sides so that it did not run through the works' precincts. Railway boats traded here with steel blooms from Stourbridge Basin. Illustrating the change that has come over the canal in the last half century or so, plans for a new 200-berth marina in the vicinity of Hinksford Lock have been passed.

Botterham Locks are a staircase pair, so remember to ensure that the top chamber is full and the bottom empty to start with. At the foot of the locks stood the Boat Inn.

Bridge Names

34 Prestwood	39 Hinksford Lock
35 Gothersley	40 Swindon
36 Flatheridge	41 Marsh
37 Greensforge	42 Botterham
38 Hinksford	

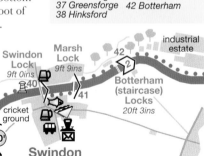

Cookley

Map 3

A village with an iron-making tradition going back three centuries and where steel wheels are still made in canalside premises. Access from the canal is via paths from either end of the tunnel.

Eating & Drinking

BULLS HEAD - Bridge Street (village centre). Tel: 01562 850242. Convivial local with a prominent outdoor terrace high above the canal. DY10 3SA

EAGLE & SPUR - Bridge Street. Tel: 01562 850184. Well appointed inn whose tables spill out on to the pavement in warm weather. DY10 3TB

A fish & chip shop (Tel: 01562 850554) and Tandoori take-away (Tel: 01562 850900) offer further options.

Shopping

Post office stores (quaint, with ham slicer, and open daily EC Wed & Sun), butcher (makes own faggots), Tesco Express (with cash machine) and florist render Cookley a useful and friendly port of call for provisions.

Connections

BUSES - Hollands service 9A runs hourly (Mon-Sat) to/from Kidderminster. Tel: 0871 200 2233.

Kinver

Map 3

Kinver is well aware of its charms and flaunts them to the full. Visitors pour in during the summer months, filling car-parks at the rear of the pubs, restaurants and cafes which provide most of the fabric of High Street. But somehow Kinver preserves its appeal and repays the ten minute stroll from the canal. In any case, the village's main asset is its superb setting in the shadow of Kinver Edge, a dramatic wooded ridge rising to five hundred feet and the southern end of the 'Staffordshire Way' long distance footpath. For those with time and energy at their disposal, the climb to the top of The Edge can be recommended. On a clear day you can see over to Bredon Hill and The Cotswolds.

Eating & Drinking

BACI - High Street. Beautifully appointed Italian restaurant. Tel: 01384 878789. DY7 6HF

HARLEYS - Dunsley Road. Tel: 01384 878899. Smokehouse grill and bar. Open Mon-Thur from noon; Fri-Sun from 9am. DY7 6LU

MANOR HOUSE - Whittington (access from Bridge 28). Tel: 01384 872110. Smartly refurbished Marston's inn/restaurant in 700 year old half-timbered property with links to Dick Whittington. DY7 6NY

PLOUGH & HARROW - High Street. Tel: 01384 872659. Unprepossessing 'local' worth patronising for the medal-winning Batham ales. DY7 6HD

SHIMLA - High Street. Tel: 01384 877744. Welcoming Indian restaurant and take-away. DY7 6HL

VINE - canalside Bridge 29. Tel: 01384 877291. Traditional pub with big garden. Food lunchtimes and evenings. Local beers - Kinver, Enville etc. DY7 6LJ

Kinver boasts many other eating & drinking establishments, from modest cafes to expensive restaurants; there are two fish & chip shops and numerous fast food outlets.

Shopping

All the shops (and there's a good choice for such an apparently small village) congregate along the High Street. Galleries and gift shops rub shoulders with a Co-op convenience store. The Butchery offers a great range of sausages and hand-raised pork pies.

Things to Do

HOLY AUSTIN ROCK HOUSES - Compton Road. Tel: 01384 872553. The National Trust have restored these typical examples of local rock houses, and they are open to the public Thursday to Sunday afternoons between March and November. Tearooms. DY7 6DL

Connections

BUSES - Hansons services 227/8 provide an hourly Mon-Sat bus link with Stourbridge. Tel: 0871 200 2233.

Swindon

Map 4

Not easily confused with its Wiltshire namesake - once you've seen it anyway - this Swindon barely amounts to more than a spattering of houses at a meeting of by-roads and a small housing estate occupying the site of a former steel works. To the west lies Highgate Common, threaded by the "Staffordshire Way", and, not far beyond - should you have the benefit of bicycles - Halfpenny Green and its vineyard.

Eating & Drinking

NAVIGATION INN - adjacent Greensforge Lock. Tel: 01384 273721. One of the most comfortable of inns on the southern half of the S&W Canal. DY6 0AH

GREEN MAN - High Street (west of Bridge 40). Tel: 01384 400532. Unspoilt village local. DY3 4NR

Another pub, cafe, and fish & chips in the village centre.

Shopping

Small convenience store and post office. SWINDON BAKERY (Tel: 01384 278861 - DY3 4NP) is a charming bakery/cafe whose hot pork rolls (and much else besides) provide a morale boost afoot or afloat.

Things to Do

ASHWOOD NURSERIES - Tel: 01384 401996. Traditional working nurseries with garden and gift shops and tea room. About 10 minutes walk from Greensforge Lock. DY6 0AE.

Summary of Facilities

Map 5

There are canalside pubs by bridges 43 and 45. The WAGGON & HORSES (Tel: 01902 892828 - WV5 0AQ) is a huge circa 1930s road house of mock half-timbering refurbished in a contemporary way. The ROUND OAK (Tel: 01902 892083 - WV5 8BU) is a Bank's all day, family oriented pub with a big canalside garden. The RAILWAY CAFE (closed Mondays) is housed in the old Wombourne station.

BELOW Bratch the canal skirts Wombourne, skirmishing with increasing amounts of housing and diminishing amounts of industry. There's a large Sainsbury's supermarket by Bridge 43. The red scars of former sand quarries abound. Narrowboats carried sand from local wharves to Black Country forges for mould making in the casting process. Bumble Hole and Bratch sound like Dickensian characters. The latter form the canal's best known locks, a trio originally built by Brindley as a staircase, but later separated and provided with extended side pounds to eliminate water waste and traffic delays. Motorised visitors to Bratch have their own car park and picnic site but, apart from a limited length of offside moorings at the foot of the flight, visitor moorings have been sacrificed for a long line of permit-holder moorings to the north.

As well as the hugely picturesque juxtaposition of the three locks, the Bratch's other attractions include an elaborately ornate pumping station dating from 1895 and a dismantled railway converted into a bridleway and public footpath. The waterworks opened in 1896, to provide supplies for Bilston near Wolverhampton, its architectural style being flamboyantly Gothic. Coal came in by narrowboat to fuel a pair of triple-expansion vertical steam engines provided by Thornewill & Warham of Burton-on-Trent. The engines, affectionately referred to as Victoria and Alexandra, fell out of use in 1960 but the former has been fully restored and the works is occasionally opened to an admiring public. The South Staffordshire Railway Walk occupies the trackbed of an old Great Western Railway line opened as late as 1925. Passenger trains lasted only seven years, but the station building at Wombourne remains intact and is used as a tea room. Wombourne village, whose delightful green - surrounded by shops and eating establishments - lies about a mile to the east, is worth seeking out if you have the time.

North of Bratch the countryside is open and attractively rolling and there are glimpses westwards of the Clee Hills. Reputedly haunted, Awbridge Lock, together with its balustraded bridge, display many of the charming characteristics of the Staffordshire & Worcestershire's engineering. A curious carving in the shape of a French man o' war, is said to date from the use of French prisoners to work on the canal following the Battle of Trafalgar.

The dock by Bridge 53 used to serve a pumping station. Now it's employed by our esteemed cover artist for the sign-writing of boats.

Bridge Names

43 Wombourne	48 Upper Bratch
44 Giggetty	49 Awbridge
45 Houndel	53 Dimmingsdale
46 Bumble Hole	54 Mops Farm
47 Bratch	55 Castle Croft

Dimmingsdale Lock 9ft 0ins

Dimmingsdale Reservoirs

Pool Hall

Ebstree Lock 9ft 0ins

Awbridge Lock 10ft 0ins

South Staffs Railway Walk

Staffordshire

Sainsbury's

43

Waggon & Horses

Bumble Hole Lock 10ft 0ins

cricket ground

Bratch Locks 30ft 2ins

70'

lock-keeper

waterworks

Wombourne (closed 1932)

Wombourne

by-roads to the centre of Wombourne

! Despite initial impressions, BRATCH LOCKS are not a 'staircase'. They are, in fact, three quite separate ordinary locks telescoped together, rendering it impossible to pass oncoming boats once they have begun to move up or down the flight. Notices regarding operation are prominently displayed. Furthermore the lock-keeper is usually in residence and dispenses milk, postcards, souvenirs and worldy wisdom from his neat octagonally shaped office on Bridge 48. At busy times do as he asks and be prepared to be patient.

WOLVERHAMPTON'S western suburbs are what estate agents would term 'residentially desirable' and they harbour little hint of Black Country industry. Moreover, the canal closets itself away from the most pressing overtures of urbanisation, masquerading its way through wooded cuttings to and from a conspirators' assignation with the Birmingham Canal Navigations at Aldersley Junction. Visitor Moorings either side of Wightwick Bridge (No.56) offer every inducement to visit the National Trust's Wightwick Manor, a late 19th Century house built for the Wolverhampton paint manufacturer Theodore Mander in beguiling Arts & Crafts style.

Evidence suggests that Compton lock was James Brindley's very first essay in narrow lock construction. The chamber is graced by one of the Staffordshire & Worcestershire Canal Society's charming wooden name posts. The lock also boasts one of the distinctive circular weirs peculiar to this canal. An impressive girder bridge carries the trackbed of the Wombourne branch railway (now a well-surfaced public right of way) over the canal on the outskirts of Tettenhall. Bridge 62B is another old railway bridge. It carried a private line into Courtaulds' long demolished rayon factory which was also served by Cowburn & Cowpar chemical boats, trading to the adjoining wharf now occupied by a community centre. Another significant canal crossing sees Bridge 62 carry Telford's Holyhead

Road. In this age of specialisation and anonymity, one can only marvel at one man's contribution to so many aspects of civil and industrial engineering. In the early years of the 19th century, communications between London and Dublin were appalling. Over twenty quite autonomous turnpike trusts were responsible for the road from London via Shrewsbury to Holyhead, the port for Ireland. Yet despite vociferous protests from travellers and the frequent failure of the Mail Coach to penetrate the wilds of Wales at all, matters were not brought to a head until the Act of Union between Britain and Ireland required the regular presence of Irish Members of Parliament at Westminster. Thomas Telford was invited to survey the route and plan improvements, which he did with characteristic thoroughness; recommending widening, resurfacing and numerous gradient modifications, as demonstrated nearby in the cutting through Tettenhall Rock. Telford's new road opened throughout with the completion of his famous bridge over the Menai Strait in 1826.

Bridge Names

56 Wightwick	61 Tettenhall Old
57 Wightwick	62 Tettenhall New
58 Wightwick Mill	62A Hordern Road
59 Compton Road	63 Dunstall Water
60 Compton Lock	64 Aldersley

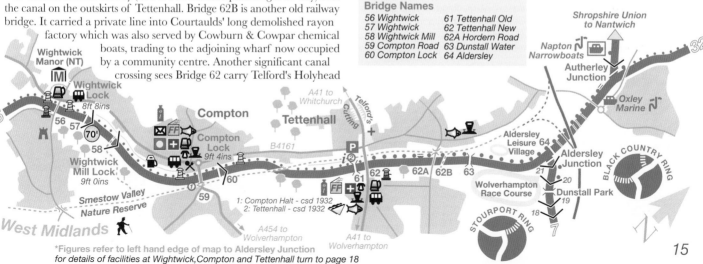

Wightwick Manor (NT)

Compton

Tettenhall

A41 to Whitchurch

Telford's Cutting

B4161

A41 to Wolverhampton

Wightwick Lock 8ft 8ins

56 57 70'

58

Wightwick Mill Lock 9ft 0ins

Smestow Valley Nature Reserve

60

59

Compton Lock 9ft 4ins

61 62 62A 62B 63

P

i

1: Compton Halt - csd 1932
2: Tettenhall - csd 1932

A454 to Wolverhampton

Shropshire Union to Nantwich

Napton Narrowboats

Autherley Junction

Oxley Marine

Aldersley Leisure Village 64

Aldersley Junction

Wolverhampton Race Course

Dunstall Park

21
20
19
18

BLACK COUNTRY RING

STOURPORT RING

7

32

West Midlands

*Figures refer to left hand edge of map to Aldersley Junction
for details of facilities at Wightwick, Compton and Tettenhall turn to page 18

15

BRINDLEY'S Birmingham Canal of 1772 encounters the proud and ancient manufacturing town of Wolverhampton. North of the town centre the canal negotiates a memorable flight of locks known colloquially as 'The Twenty-one'. At its foot lies an unexpectedly rural junction with the Staffordshire & Worcestershire Canal at Aldersley: an appropriately bosky name. There is so much to see that the flight never becomes tedious. The 'Twenty-one' is well maintained and seems somehow less exhausting than one might expect. Brindley only provided twenty chambers, but the last was so deep that it caused water shortages. In 1784 the bottom lock was therefore reduced in depth and a short cutting excavated to carry the canal to a new lock built in the intervening pound. This extra lock - No.20 - gives its identity away by having only one bottom gate.

In working boat days the locks were the haunt of 'hobblers', men or boys who would help single-handed captains through the locks for a small consideration: occasionally, latter-day hobblers are on hand to provide the same service. Another feature of the flight were boat children apparently in the habit of riding horses bareback, at breakneck speed down to Aldersley to collect upcoming boats. Galloping equines are still encountered on the flight in the slightly different form of

thoroughbreds on the neighbouring race course; a rare juxtaposition - one can only think of Aintree and Ripon in comparison.

McDonald's offer the opportunity for lock-wheelers to take some sustenance on board at Gorsebrook Bridge, as does a mobile catering van by Fox's Lane Bridge. A Science Park borders the canal between locks 12 to 15 where Clayton tar boats used to ply to and from the gas works. Wolverhampton has always been a fascinating railway centre, and the once rival lines of the Great Western and London Midland & Scottish railways span the canal at several points, notably on a pair of fine viaducts. Lock 11 must have been a trainspotter's idea of heaven when the best of Swindon and Crewe puffed imperiously overhead. Between locks 9 and 10 the pit of an old turntable can still be discovered in the undergrowth on the towpath side. Here stood the coaling stage of Stafford Road engine shed, home to a number of the Great Western Railway's legendary King and Castle classes of express locomotives.

Wolverhampton's refuse incinerator - incongruously juxtaposed with

Key 1
1 site of Stafford Road rly wks
2 rems of Springfield Brewery
3 former GWR goods depot
4 Broad Street depot (FMC)
5 Low Level Station (GWR)
6 Chubb Works
7 disused corn/flour mill
8 site of LNWR/LMS railway basin
9 Albion Wharf
10 Wulfruna Coal Co.
11 former power station
12 Chillington Wharf (Monmore Green)

Boaters require 'water conservation' handcuff keys to access paddle gear on the Wolverhampton locks.

a banqueting suite - overlooks the middle of the flight. The imposing Springfield Brewery of 1873 - 'Home of Butlers Ales - Pride of the Midlands' - has been almost irretrievably damaged by fire, but is worth walking down Grimstone Street to view at closer quarters. Locks 2 and 3 are overlooked by the corrugated-iron-clad premises of a builders merchant which originally housed an extensive Great Western Railway goods depot.*

Above the top lock - with its weeping willows, rabbit holes and picturesque pair of BCN cottages - the canal widens into a landscaped area where fairly salubrious visitor moorings are provided for overnight stops. The present Broad Street bridge replaces an earlier structure that boasted cast-iron balustrades and ornate gas lamps and which now graces the Black Country Living Museum. The adjoining warehouse was owned by the famous canal carriers, Fellows, Morton & Clayton. Water, Elsan and refuse disposal facilities are obtainable by entering a short arm spanned by a cast iron bridge immediately south of Broad Street Bridge. More visitor moorings are provided on the opposite side to the towpath at this point: hard-by the busy ring-road, they offer an enhanced sense of security at the expense of access to or from the outside world. The arm was the original course of the canal before it was diverted through Wolverhampton Tunnel when the High Level railway station was built in 1850. Above the tunnel there's a multi-storey car park for rail users. It is said that Wolverhampton's 'ladies of the night' were in the habit of entertaining their customers in the twilight of the canal tunnel. Like a sizeable wedge of chocolate cake, Chubb's former lock and safe-making works dominates the horizon.

*Also destroyed by fire, Leap Year's Day, 2012.

Hoodie or Hobbler?

Springfield Brewery

Beyond Mill Street Bridge, a former canal warehouse at Albion Wharf has been converted into apartments and finds itself crowded-in on by spanking new flats as if it were a defiant pensioner surrounded by taunting 'hoodies'. At Horseley Fields Junction the Wyrley & Essington Canal commences its tortuous circumnavigation of the north-western tip of the Black Country - turn to Map 35 to learn how it gets on. Nearby, Wulfruna Coal Merchants establish a degree of retro atmosphere. Long ago they operated their own coal boats. Nowadays the yard provides a base for a Community Payback vessel, aboard which young offenders tour the local canals doing penance by cleaning them up: today's petty criminals, tomorrow's canal activists?

The emerging railways of the mid 19th century quickly grasped that development of short haul traffic, to and from the numerous works firmly established beside the densely knit canals, was in their best interest. One, of what amounted to over forty, railway owned basins, remains intact at Chillington Wharf and has been given Grade II listed status, though each time we pass looks a bit sorrier for itself. It's one thing 'listing' buildings, quite another maintaining them.

South of Wolverhampton the BCN's main line pursues a winding course. Improved access at bridges has been undertaken to encourage walkers and cyclists onto the towpath. Bilston Road Bridge carries the Metro tramway across the canal. At Rough Hills Stop the canal narrows at the site of a former toll house and there are more BCN cottages.

Wightwick
Map 6

Wolverhampton's most westerly suburb. Sneeze and you're in Staffordshire!

Eating & Drinking
THE MERMAID - adjacent Bridge 56. Tel: 01902 764896. Picturesque road side pub dating from 18th Century and now part of the Vintage Inns group. Open daily from noon. WV6 8BN

Things to Do
WIGHTWICK MANOR - Wightwick Bank. Tel: 01902 761400. Sublime late Victorian house furnished by the Arts & Crafts movement: Morris, Rossetti, Kempe, Burne-Jones et al. In the words of the National Trust Handbook: 'A time capsule of Victorian nostalgia for medieval England'. Extensive gardens, tea room (using kitchen garden produce) and National Trust gift shop specialising in William Morris ranges. WV6 8EE

Compton
Map 6

Another of Wolverhampton's suburban outposts and location of the Wanderers training ground.

Eating & Drinking
FIUME - Bridgnorth Road (canalside Bridge 59). Tel: 01902 618749. Italian restaurant. WV6 8AB
Pizza Hut, Indian, Chinese, two pubs and fish & chips also within east reach of the canal.

Shopping
Spar (including post office and cash machine), pharmacy and launderette, but sadly the DAISY ('Fresh & Essential') food store, which so impressed us previously, has regressed into a Sainsbury's Local.

Tettenhall
Map 6

Outlier of Wolverhampton which still displays a rural feel and, possibly uniquely, *two* village greens. The former railway station (which retains its buildings, platforms and goods shed) is employed as a Ranger's Office for the Smestow Valley (linear) Nature Reserve.

Wolverhampton

Wolverhampton
Map 7

Wolverhampton reminds us of Wakefield, another proud and ancient borough, linked to the inland waterways, but apt to languish in the shadows of a domineering neighbour: in Wakefield's case, Leeds, in Wolverhampton's ... well, no names no packdrill! Both cities have had to come to terms with the erosion of heavy industry and to find sustainable uses for weighty legacies of flamboyant Victorian and Edwardian buildings. But Wulfrunians can console themselves that their pedigree is more impressive than that of the upstart down the A41; why they even installed the country's first traffic lights as early as 1927.

Eating & Drinking
GREAT WESTERN - Sun Street. Tel: 01902 351090. Splendid establishment! Railway and football memorabilia, Holdens, Bathams, guest beers, Black Country cooking at lunchtimes: grey peas & bacon, hot pork cobs, faggots & chips, fish pies etc. WV10 0DJ

THE BLUEBRICK - Sun Street. Tel: 01902 875301. Bistro and bar incorporated within fabric of old Low Level railway station and operated as part of Whitbread's 'Table Table' chain. WV10 0DJ
CATELLANI'S - School Street. Tel: 01902 428928. Super little Italian restaurant. Quite a find for Wolverhampton! From noon daily, ex Sun. WV1 4LR

Shopping
The Mander and Wulfrun centres are modern precincts emblazoning all the inevitable names in plastic facia. But down side streets and up alleyways plenty of characterful local shops are waiting to be discovered by the discerning shopper. Wolverhampton Books & Collectibles occupy a 17th century timber-framed building on the corner of Victoria Street and St Johns Street. There's a lively retail market on Tue, Wed, Fri & Sat and a Farmers' Market on the first and third Fridays of the month. Beatties art deco department store recalls a more gracious shopping epoch.

Things to Do
ART GALLERY - Lichfield Street. Tel: 01902 552055. Dignified Italianate building dating from the 1880s; note how the first floor is windowless, because, of course, the wall space was required for hanging paintings which are top lit from the roof. Look out for the work of Edwin Butler Bayliss (1874-1950) who captured the industrial Black Country to a T. Local tourist information and excellent cafe. WV1 1DU
ST PETER'S CHURCH - Lichfield Street. Tel: 01902 422642. Imposing collegiate church in red sandstone. Visitor Centre featuring local history. Shop. WV1 1TY

Connections
BUSES - West Midlands hub. Tel: 0871 200 2233.
TRAINS - busy railhead. Tel: 08457 484950.
TRAMS - Treat yourself to a ride on the Metro, a fascinating journey across what's left of the industrial Black Country and the opportunity to eavesdrop on oral history in the making as you go along!
TAXIS - Associated. Tel: 01902 420420.

S O what do you think of it so far? - the BCN that is. Are you under its spell, or are you under psychoanalysis, still hyperventilating from its fulminating blend of inspirational post-industrial heritage and sheer downright ugliness? Love it, or loathe it, you're here now, so make the most of the BCN's Main Line as, between Wolverhampton and Tipton, in sinuous accord with the contours, it betrays its Brindley origins. Only on the cut through Coseley - engineered by Thomas Telford to by-pass the circuitous Wednesbury Oak Loop (partially retained to serve the lock-gate workshops at Bradley) - do 19th century improvements deviate from the original route of 1772. And if you are prepared to use your imagination, there will barely be a dull moment as the canal traverses an area of the Black Country where the traditional activities of the

region have been replaced by ubiquitous industrial units and innocuous housing estates. You are a symptom of this change. The relative popularity of boating, walking and cycling the BCN is largely a recent phenomenon, helped no little, in the first case, by the popularity of the "Stourport Ring". The recreational potential of canals, however, was recognised too late to save approximately one third of the BCN system from being abandoned during the Fifties and Sixties.

Demolition continues to take its toll of the Black Country's latent atmosphere. In the quarter of a century that we have been familiar with the BCN some iconic canalside premises have vanished. The site of Beans Foundry is an unappealing wasteland of rubble. In the Twenties, Beans rivalled Ford in the realms of affordable motoring for the masses. In 1938 their specially constructed 'Thunderbolt' broke the land speed record, achieving 357 mph at Bonneville, USA. Utilitarian nomenclature abounds on the BCN, and at Factory Junction, Brindley's "Wolverhampton Level" and Telford's "Birmingham Level" are seen to meet or divide, depending on your direction of travel. Boating towards Birmingham you have a choice (always assuming both routes are free of

continued on page 21:

Map labels:

Loxdale · Bradley Lane · Metro · Pot House · Bilston Church · Glasshouse · Banks · Bradley · Bradley Workshops · crse of GWR · Wolverhampton-Stourbridge · 70' · Highfields Rd. · Millfields Road · Jibbet Lane · Catchem's Corner · 7 · Ten Score · Anchor · 1 · DEEPFIELDS JUNCTION · Hills · Deepfields · North Coseley · Coseley · Coseley Tunnel 360 yards · Wall-brook · A4123 · Bloomfield Junction · 2 · Factory Locks 20ft 0ins · FACTORY JUNCTION · Caggy's · Watery Lane · Tipton · TIPTON JUNCTION · Pitch-fork · 9a · 9b · A457 · The Portal (DC&TT) Dudley Tunnel 3172yrds · Black Country Living Museum · 3 4

Key 1
1 site of Bilston Steelworks
2 site of Beans Foundry
3 site of LNWR basin
4 site of GWR basin
5 former Boatmen's Mission
6 former gauging dock
7 Malthouse Stables

***No locks on Old Main Line route**

for details of facilities at Tipton turn to page 20

Tipton

Map 8

Back when the Tipton Green & Toll End Communication Canal was 'in water', Tipton was literally islanded by canals and had been comically compared with Venice long before the analogy was poached by Birmingham. With its early car production line, soap, lubricants, blue bricks and sausage manufactures, Tipton had always punched economically above its weight, so it is appropriate that the little town's most famous son was William Perry aka 'The Tipton Slasher', England's champion prizefighter for seven undefeated years from 1850. His pugilistic years followed a period as a canal boatman; ideal preparation one imagines. Another sporting claim to fame is that of Tipton Harriers, the athletics club which celebrated its centenary in 2010. Their most notable exponent was Jack Holden who won Commonwealth and European gold medals for the marathon in 1950, thus covering the club - whose motto is 'Swift & Eager' - in a reflected glory never quite shaken off. Tipton Library features an excellent little Heritage Centre.

Eating & Drinking

MAD O'ROURKE'S PIE FACTORY - Hurst Lane. Tel: 0121 557 1402. Eccentric street corner pub recently resurrected and once again serving its gargantuan Desperate Dan Pies and Lump Hammer Ale. DY4 9AB

Shopping

Handy shops easily reached from either of the main lines, though the only cash machine we could find was *inside* the post office. Small market on Tuesdays.

Things to Do

BLACK COUNTRY LIVING MUSEUM - Tipton Road, Dudley. Tel: 0121 557 9643. Admission charge. With each new edition of this guide, the disparity grows between the real West Midlands and this little pocket of it, preserved in aspic on a 26 acre site. It will take you at

BCLM

least a couple of hours to walk around the exhibits which include a village, colliery, pumping engine, boat dock and fairground. Rolfe Street Baths (which used to overlook the canal as it passed so dramatically through Smethwick) have been re-erected here as an excellent exhibition hall devoted to Black Country social history and industrial archaeology. Trams (and sometimes - even more enticingly - trolleybuses) offer rides from the main entrance to the village. Secure moorings (with comprehensive facilities) are available for visiting boaters, access via Tipton Junction. Refreshments include a Canalside Cafe, Fried Fish Shop (where the fish & chips are cooked as per local tradition in beef-dripping) and the Bottle & Glass Inn.

Frankly, it would be ludicrous to boat along the BCN Main Line and not call in here. DY1 4SQ DUDLEY CANAL & TUNNEL TRUST - Birmingham New Road. Tel: 0121 557 6265. 45 minute boat trips from the imposing new Portal Visitor Centre into Dudley Tunnel and its fabulous limestone caverns. Longer trips through the entire length of the tunnel, and also Netherton Tunnel on selected dates. DY1 4SB

Connections

BUSES - links from centre of Tipton to/from Dudley (an interesting town with a zoo (and castle) to visit) also calling at stops by the Black Country Living Museum, otherwise about 20 minutes walk from the railway station. Tel: 0871 200 2233.

TRAINS - local services half-hourly between Wolverhampton and Birmingham. Tel: 03457 484950.

TAXIS - 121 Cars. Tel: 0121 557 1557.

Bradley

Map 8

Enclaves of housing, peppered with pockets of light industry, characterise this corner of the Black Country now, but there is much for the diligent canal explorer to discover. The Bradley Branch of the Wednesbury Oak Loop, for example, can be followed on foot down to Moorcroft Junction - Map 41. Bradley Workshops - whose resinous aromas waft over the canal - continue to output upwards of a hundred lock-gates per annum, but the staff are down to about a dozen and the fleet of maintenance craft, latterly resident here, have all gone, drastically reducing boat passages on what is left of the Wednesbury Oak Loop.

Eating & Drinking

Fish & chips. The White Hart, up from Pothouse Bridge, serves Black Country Ales, but *not* food.

Shopping

Convenience store with post office counter near Glasshouse Bridge. Ditto adjacent to terminus.

continued from page 19:

stoppages) between the directness of Telford's wide, embanked, twin-towpathed 'Island Line', twenty feet below through the three Factory Locks, and Brindley's original route which parallels it, hugging the 473ft contour in the shadow of the Rowley Hills. The former, accompanied by the busy railway, encounters Caggy's boatyard, named after Caggy Stevens, the BCN's last working boatman. The latter affords access to the Black Country Living Museum, where secure overnight moorings and boating facilities are available in the surreal environs of a 19th century time warp. Incorporated into the museum, an unusual vertical lift bridge (rescued from the Great Western Railway's Tipton interchange basin), gives access to a section of Lord Ward's Canal which led directly from the Old Main Line to a bank of lime kilns which still forms an attractive feature of the museum. Several historic boats are usually on display here, and there is a working boat dock where visitors can see some of the trades and techniques of Black Country boat construction taking place.

Beyond the museum moorings is the northern portal of Dudley Tunnel, first dug in 1775 to gain access to subterranean limestone workings. Ten years later it was extended through to join up with the Dudley Canal at Park Head (Map 34). The sole preserve of electrically-powered trip boats for many years, Dudley Tunnel re-opened to general boating traffic in 1992, with the proviso that they be shafted and 'legged' through so as to avoid the creation of engine fumes, and that they meet the fairly restrictive gauge limitations. Since then, life has been made easier by the introduction of a tug to haul you through: contact the Dudley Canal Trust (Tel: 0121 557 6265 - *www.dudleycanaltrust.org.uk*) for more details.

By Factory Junction (named after the long vanished Borax soap works) two interesting buildings survive. Between the pub and the top lock a former Boatmen's Mission now finds use as a workshop making ornamental ironwork. This was one of five such establishments on the BCN dispensing hot drinks, tobacco, washing facilities and a little transitory warmth and companionship. On the Sabbath the emphasis became more overtly religious, and Sunday School lessons were held for boat children. On the opposite bank of the top lock stands a former BCN gauging station where the carrying capacity of boats was calculated for toll taking purposes. Craft gained access through two arches at the west end of the

building. Recently, this listed and hugely significant structure has been placed in jeopardy by a proposal that the site be cleared for a housing development. Perhaps it would be sensible to move it, brick by brick, to the safety of the Black Country Living Museum.

Beyond the junction, in the direction of Wolverhampton and on the far side of the modern road bridge, lay the entrance to the Great Western Railway basin. Railway owned boats would operate between these interchange points and 'boatage' depots which were wharves operated by the railways but without direct rail links. The London & North Western Railway also had an extensive interchange basin at nearby Bloomfield. Back at the junction, alongside the Old Main Line's route, former malthouse stables have been given a new lease of life as a canoe centre - boaters should proceed with due care. Snaking round the corner, past The Fountain public house and under Owen Street Bridge, Brindley's route skirts the centre of Tipton, passing a small park where the local authority have erected a statue of William Perry, aka 'the Tipton Slasher. More to the BCN than you thought? You've barely scratched the surface, chum!

The Wednesbury Oak Loop

The new route opened in 1837 between Deepfields and Bloomfield junctions was just over a mile long, yet it replaced something like four miles of typical Brindley wanderings which then became known as the Wednesbury Oak Loop. Largely abandoned by 1960, a mile and a half remains in use from Deepfields connecting Bradley (pronounced with a flat 'a', as in what donkeys do) lock-gate manufacturing workshops with the main line, an all too tempting diversion for those enamoured of backwaters. From the outset a real sense of exploration is engendered: the margins are reedy; the water turquoise coloured; whilst tethered ponies dolefully regard your passing, as if to say: "you need your heads seeing to". Much of the BCN's water supply, pumped from old mine workings, reaches the main line along this weedy conduit. On the wall of the pumping house at the end of the canal a plaque recalls the bizarre deaths of Maud and Frederick Fellows here on the 31st January 1916, killed by 'enemy action' when a passing Zeppelin dropped a bomb on them.

Stourport Ring

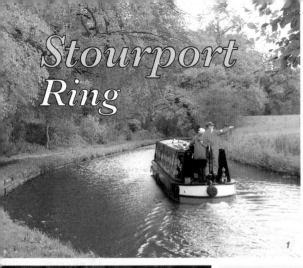

1 Kinver
2 Birmingham
3 Bilston Coot
4 Worcester
5 Cookley
6 Titford Mallards

1 Tibberton Top
2 Horseley Fields
3 The Bratch
4 Galton Bridge
5 Dunhampstead
6 Engine Arm Aqueduct
7 Coseley Tunnel

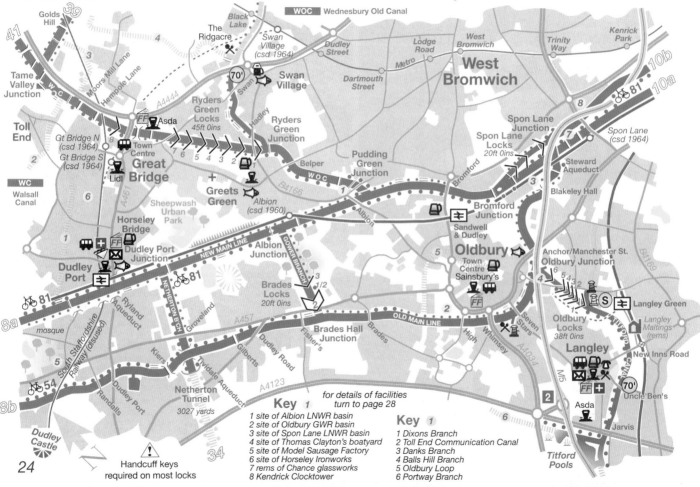

WOC Wednesbury Old Canal

Golds Hill

39
41

The Ridgacre

Black Lake

Swan Village (csd 1964)

Swan Village

Dudley Street

Lodge Road

West Bromwich

Trinity Way

Kenrick Park

10b
10a
81

Tame Valley Junction

Moors Mill Lane

Hempole Lane

70'

Swan

Hadley

Ryders Green Locks 45ft 0ins

Ryders Green Junction

Dartmouth Street

Metro

West Bromwich

8

Spon Lane Junction

Spon Lane Locks 20ft 0ins

7

Spon Lane (csd 1964)

Steward Aqueduct

Toll End

Asda
FF

Gt Bridge N (csd 1964)

Gt Bridge S (csd 1964)

Town Centre

Great Bridge

Lidl

A461

A4444

Belper

B4166

WOC

Pudding Green Junction

Albion

Bromford

Bromford Junction

Blakeley Hall

3

WC Walsall Canal

6

Sheepwash Urban Park

Greets Green

Albion (csd 1960)

Albion Junction

Sandwell & Dudley

Oldbury

5

Anchor/Manchester St. Oldbury Junction

B4169

Horseley Bridge

FF

Dudley Port Junction

1

NEW MAIN LINE

GOWER BRANCH

Brades Locks 20ft 0ins

3
1/2
2

Town Centre Sainsbury's

FF

4

6 5 4 3 2

Oldbury Locks 38ft 0ins

S

1

Langley Green

Dudley Port

81

Ryland Aqueduct

NETHERTON BCH

81

8a

mosque

South Staffordshire Railway (disused)

Groveland

Kiers

Dudley Port

Tividale Aqueduct

Brades Hall Junction

Fisher's

Gilberts

Dudley Road

Brades

OLD MAIN LINE

A457

High

Whimsey

Seven Stars

A4034

M5

4

Langley Maltings (rems)

New Inns Road

Langley

70'

FF

Uncle Ben's

8b

54
81

Randalls

Netherton Tunnel 3027 yards

A4123

2

6

Asda

Jarvis

Dudley Castle

N

⚠ Handcuff keys required on most locks

Key 1
1 site of Albion LNWR basin
2 site of Oldbury GWR basin
3 site of Spon Lane LNWR basin
4 site of Thomas Clayton's boatyard
5 site of Model Sausage Factory
6 site of Horseley Ironworks
7 rems of Chance glassworks
8 Kendrick Clocktower

for details of facilities turn to page 28

Key 1
1 Dixons Branch
2 Toll End Communication Canal
3 Danks Branch
4 Balls Hill Branch
5 Oldbury Loop
6 Portway Branch

Titford Pools

34

ZEALOUS canal explorers are spoilt for choice as the old and new main lines of the Birmingham Canal Navigations pursue their respective - and intrinsically distinct - courses between Tipton and Smethwick. Twice the routes are interconnected (*thrice* if you are walking or cycling the towpath), creating a series of mini-rings within rings, a temptation to go round and round in ever decreasing circles. And there are junctions beckoning to branches remote, even by BCN standards, not least the splendid and challenging Titford Canal.

The Old Main Line

Brindley's route tends to be less boated than Telford's. Duckweed encroaches on the channel whilst moorhens and coots are confident enough in being undisturbed to build precarious nests midstream. East of Tipton the Old Main Line (aka the Wolverhampton Level) runs through council housing, passes beneath the mothballed South Staffordshire Railway - long ago earmarked for re-opening as part of the Metro tramway system - then finds itself in the much changed environment of 'Tividale Quays', a housing development incorporating a large canal basin, underlining the significant role that the BCN has played in the regeneration and 'greening' of the new Black Country; though there will be some who feel that a considerable amount of character has been lost in the process. If this feeling of being short-changed applies to you, then you need to get yourself down to the reference library and study old, large scale maps of the area to grasp the hive of industry which once existed here. Trace the Wolverhampton Level's route past colliery basins, iron foundry basins and brick-works basins and you begin to gain some conception of the canal's former pre-eminence.

Tividale Aqueduct carries the old main line over the Netherton Tunnel Branch. There is no waterway connection here, but a path links the two levels. Netherton's northern portal looks intriguing and sepulchral when seen from the vantage point of the aqueduct, as though it might somehow lead you into the past, if only you had the courage to go there. At Brades Hall Junction the Gower Branch descends through the BCN's solitary 'staircase' lock to join Telford's main line, half a mile to the north. There are occasional glimpses south towards the Rowley Hills and Dudley Castle.

The canal's original route through Oldbury was even more convoluted. Oldbury Junction (egress point of the Titford Canal) suffers the indignity of being located beneath the M5 motorway. This was the site (between 1935 and 1966) of a boatyard belonging to another carrying company inseparable from the history of this area's canals. Thomas Clayton specialised in the transport of bulk liquids. With a fleet in excess of eighty boats to maintain, this yard presented a busy scene, a distinctive aspect of which were two mobile slipway shelters which provided some protection from the weather while craft were being repaired. Clayton's best known long distance traffic was the carriage of oil from Ellesmere Port to Shell's depot at Langley Green, a contract which lasted from 1924 until 1955; some of the boats remaining horse-drawn until virtually the end.

Southwards from Oldbury, Clayton boats - with their distinctive decked holds and river names - served gasworks at Oxford, Banbury, Leamington and Solihull, but the bulk of their trade was of a more localised nature, notably the carriage of gas works by-products such as tar. Their last cargo - carried aboard the now preserved motor *Stour* - arrived at Midland Tar Distillers, Oldbury from Walsall Gasworks on 31st March 1966. Faced with diminishing cargoes (brought about largely by the advent of North Sea gas) and the disruption brought about by construction of the elevated section of the M5, Thomas Clayton called it a day. The contemporary face of transportation manifests itself nearby in the shape of a vast road-based distribution hub: *Sic Transport Gloria Mundi*

Playing hopscotch with the elevated motorway, the old main line proceeds towards Smethwick. Blakeley Hall Bridge possibly recalls the existence of some long-vanished mansion. The simple, hump-backed character of the bridge contrasts starkly with the overhanging motorway's concrete ceiling. In dramatic sequence, the canal passes beneath the Birmingham to Wolverhampton railway, crosses Telford's route by way of Steward Aqueduct, and meets Brindley's original route to Wednesbury at Spon Lane Junction. The aqueduct's impact is somewhat diluted by the hefty pillars of the motorway towering above it. Interestingly, the iron lattice footbridge immediately south of the railway is numbered as a railway and not canal structure, undoubtedly because it was part of the adjoining interchange basin with the London & North Western Railway.

continued overleaf:

continued from page 25:
The New Main Line

Whilst Brindley's canal winds about the foot of the Rowley Hills reciting metaphysical poetry to itself, Telford's gets to grips with the business of reaching Birmingham in a no nonsense manner which accountants would approve of. For almost three miles the canal runs as true as a line on a balance sheet, crossing great open expanses of wasteground where large craters recall past quarrying and brickmaking. These areas have been redeveloped as urban woodland. Inexorably the Black Country is becoming green again, going full circle back to its pre-industrial innocence.

Junction after junction - some vanished, some intact - keep the adrenalin flowing. The short Dixon's Branch served the Horseley Iron Works foundry which moved from its earlier site at Tipton in 1865. Three aqueducts carry the canal across two roads and a railway. The most notable, Ryland Aqueduct, is a concrete rebuilding of 1968. A short loop railway once crossed the canal here, used by the 'Dudley Dodger' push & pull train which ran from the town station at Dudley to connect with main line trains at Dudley Port. The rusty, overgrown tracks of the old South Staffordshire Railway are all a far cry from the days when Palethorpe's nearby 'sausage siding' was shunted on a daily basis.

At Dudley Port Junction the Netherton Branch makes a bee-line for its famous tunnel. Opened in 1858 to relieve pressure on the parallel Dudley Tunnel route, it was the last canal tunnel to be built in Britain, going into the record books - at 3027 yards - as the eighth longest. Subsequent closures have rendered it fourth only (in navigable terms) to Standedge on the Huddersfield Narrow Canal, Dudley itself, and Blisworth on the Grand Union.

Trainspotting becomes second nature by the time you reach Albion Junction, where the Gower Branch links up with the old main line and 'Wolverhampton Level'. A former toll island all but fills the width of the new main line; an 'eye of the needle' job for nervous steerers. Two more junctions tempt you in quick succession. From Pudding Green the door swings open to the under-boated waters of the 'northern half' of the BCN via Brindley's original Wednesbury Canal, whilst at Bromford Junction there's a link with the old main line through the trio of Spon Lane Locks. These locks are quite possibly the oldest working chambers in the country, and enjoy listed status. Here, between 1861 and 1890 the evangelist John Skidmore held weekly, open air revivalist meetings each summer, with attendances peaking at an incredible twenty thousand souls. According to Skidmore's diaries, the throngs assembled on slag heaps bordering the middle lock. 'Thousands worshipped God in the open air ... rich and poor, old and young, well-dressed and ragged, drapers, grocers, butchers, tailors, publicans, ironmasters, clerks, magistrates, puddlers, coalmasters, mine agents, colliers, navvies, boatmen, roadmen, labourers, sweeps, a goodly number of Frenchmen from the Glass House (Chances - see below), the aged and infirm, the lame and the blind, men of all creeds and no creed at all.' Skidmore had been inspired to hold meetings when, whilst out distributing tracts, he had come upon a gathering of colliers and ironworkers at Spon Lane engaged in cockfighting and dog-fighting, gambling and whippet-racing. Through sheer force of personality the then youthful missionary persuaded these rough diamonds to attend an evangelist meeting on the spot the following Sunday. The meetings continued for nearly thirty years until the canal company reclaimed this lawless land. Negotiating the flight now, you need all the imagination you can muster to visualize the al fresco congregation, moved, in turn, to laughter and tears by Skidmore's oratory. There must have been times when they made as much noise as the crowd at West Bromwich Albion's nearby Hawthorns football ground. Nowadays the noise comes from the incessant roar of traffic on the elevated section of the M5 motorway. The top lock is all but engulfed by the road, its tiny, cantilevered, cast iron tail bridge provoking piquant contrast with the motorway's massive concrete pillars and girders.

Meanwhile Telford's route keeps to the 'Birmingham Level' and passes beneath the M5 and Steward Aqueduct, entering a vast cutting of blue-brick retaining walls between the railway on one side and the crumbling remains of what's left of Chance's glassworks on the other. The works, which in its heyday lined both sides of the canal and railway (hence the linking arches which appear superfluous now) was known world-wide as a manufacturer of, amongst many other things, glass for lighthouses. A Heritage Lottery funded website, punningly known as *Chance Encounters*, celebrates the heritage of the firm.

The Wednesbury 'Old' Canal

Pudding Green ought to be the name of some picturesque village snuggled deep in the Sussex Weald. Instead, it's an incongruous gateway to and from the northern waters of the BCN; though we did discover wild poppies and lupins flowering bravely along the towpath yards from the junction itself. But flora and fauna - other than the ubiquitous rosebay willowherb and the geese which appear to be Canada's greatest export - are otherwise none too conspicuous as the canal winds through an area of metal and chemical works past the site of the old Albion railway basin; the inspiration for an atmospheric night-time interior painting by Brian Collings included as a plate in Tom Foxon's evocative memoirs of a working boatman *Number One*. Reference to the Godfrey Edition Ordnance Survey reprint for Greets Green in 1902 illustrates the layout of Albion Basin and, indeed, the full course of the Wednesbury Old Canal to its present truncated terminus at Swan Bridge. Though not as built upon as now, the canal's course is accompanied by numerous side basins and arms - twenty or more at a rough count - emphasising the canal's vital role in the industrialisation process of an area of once wild heathland.

At Ryders Green Junction the Walsall Canal descends through a flight of eight locks to Great Bridge. Veering to the right, Brindley's original canal carries on for another half mile or so to Swan Bridge until petering out where the Black Country Spine Road controversially - in canal circles at any rate - brought about closure of the canal. Historically the canal continued from here to Swan Bridge Junction where one arm, known as the Balls Hill Branch, wound its way to Hill Top, terminating amidst colliery shafts beside the Holyhead Road. A second arm, called the Ridgacre Branch - trifurcated into the long forgotten Dartmouth, Halford and Jesson extremities. This is a real backwater, a reclusive enclave of bullrush-encroached canal inhabited, solely it seems, by herons, coots ... and itinerant guide book compilers. Wisdom suggests it is not safe to approach any of these categories.

The Titford Canal

Half a dozen locks - nicknamed 'The Crow' - lift the Titford up to its 511ft height above sea level, nowadays the BCN's loftiest pound. The chambers have single-leaf gates at both top and tail, and the short intervening pounds feature extended side ponds to increase water capacity. With no reservoir, as such, to feed its summit, the Titford Canal relies largely on pumping and precipitation to maintain a navigable depth.

The canal's surroundings are overwhelmingly industrial, whilst an acrid smell - part chemical, part burnt offering - seems to hang permanently over the proceedings. A refurbished engine house (used as an appropriate meeting room by the Birmingham Canal Navigations Society) marks the junction with the old Tat Bank Branch, now replete with moorings and boating facilities, its far end an unlikely sanctuary for water voles.

Passing under the Great Western Railway's Langley Green-Oldbury branchline (closed to passengers as long ago as the First World War, though comparatively recently to goods) you reach the skeletal remains of Langley Maltings, destroyed by fire in 2009. Though Grade II listed, they had ceased being used three years earlier and plans for redevelopment had stalled. An iconic Black Country building by any standards, its destruction is nothing short of tragedy. Barley used to be brought in by boat.

By Uncle Ben's Bridge, Slade's Coal Wharf was supplied by boat until 1967. A neat little park (from which the strains of the prize-winning

Langley Band are sometimes to be heard) precedes a length of canal embalmed in suburbia before the junction of the old Portway and Causeway Green branch canals (gradually abandoned between 1954 and 1960) heralds the end of navigation; a rather eldritch, road-noisy terminus if the truth were known. Intrepid boaters can toy with exploration of the coot-haunted, debris-filled Titford Pools, navigating beneath the cylindrical concrete support columns of the M5 motorway; though there are treacherous shallows to contend with, together with terrapins if not crocodiles.

Oldbury   Map 9

"Of Oldbury, with its mean, blackened streets, I can find no redeeming words to say." That was L. T. C. Rolt's considered opinion in 1949, and there will be those who wouldn't argue with it now. No longer in Worcestershire, redevelopment has radically botoxed the town's face, and since 1974 it has been the seat of power in the Metropolitan Borough of Sandwell: the council's pagoda-like headquarters dominate the town. The new library is housed in a building named after Jack Judge, music hall entertainer and composer of *It's A Long Way to Tipperary*, who was born in the town in 1872.

Eating & Drinking

VALENCIA WHARF COFFEE SHOP - Whimsey Bridge. Tel: 0121 544 6794. Annex to aquatic garden centre. Breakfasts, coffees/teas, lunches. B69 2AP
COURT OF REQUESTS - Church Street. Tel: 0121 543 6970. Wetherspoons housed in a handsome building which was originally a court room, but more recently the town's library before it moved - see above. Open daily from 7am. B69 3AF

Shopping

Oldbury offers the best canalside choice in shops between Wolverhampton and Birmingham, though there are no formal visitor moorings. The centre is most easily reached from the Old Main Line, but is also little more than half a mile from Telford's route at Bromford. Sainsbury's supermarket near Whimsey Bridge.

Connections

BUSES - frequent links with Dudley, Birmingham etc. Tel: 0871 200 2233.
TRAINS - Sandwell & Dudley railhead by Bromford Bridge on New Main Line. Tel: 03457 484950.
TAXIS - Apollo. Tel: 0121 557 1500.

Great Bridge   Map 9

The Spine Road has brought 21st century mundanity to Great Bridge - would that Giuseppe Bonaccorsi's horse-drawn Italian ice cream carts still patrolled the neighbourhood - but there are still overtones of durable Black Country character, and Great Bridge remains a more than useful frontier post for stocking up on life's little luxuries before heading off into the barbarous northern wastes of the BCN.

Eating & Drinking

THE EIGHT LOCKS - canalside top of Ryder's Green Locks. Tel: 0121 522 3800. Food, pool, darts, televised sports and a beer garden. B70 0AN
THE RIDGACRE - overlooking Swan Bridge Junction. Tel: 08701 977 264. Table Table bar/restaurant. B70 0NP
Fish & chips from Frydays or The Black Country Chippy. McDonald's and KFC drive-thrus.

Shopping

Access between locks 7 and 8 to main thoroughfare of shops, Asda supermarket and Boots pharmacy. Small retail markets Weds & Sats.

Connections

BUSES - service 74 operates at frequent intervals to/from Dudley, West Bromwich and Birmingham, connecting with the nearest railhead at Dudley Port. Tel: 0871 200 2233.
METRO - handy pedestrian access from Black Lake station to isolated section of Ridgacre Branch.
TAXIS - West Brom Cars. Tel: 0121 553 5050.

Langley   Map 9

The Black Country's pulse still beats faintly in little communities like Langley. It feels just like a village; albeit a village surrounded by chemical and plastics plants. There are two convenience stores, a post office, a newsagent and a pharmacy. But our favourite is Mellors, specialists in shoe repairs, hiking and walking boots.

The Teapot cafe does filling breakfasts, and there's also a small bakers and several Indian takeaways. Entertainment - in addition to exploration of the Titford Canal - is provided by the Oldbury Repertory Players at their Barlow Theatre. Telephone the Box Office for performance details on 0121 552 2761.

Connections

BUSES - service 120 operates quarter-hourly (hourly Sun) to/ from Birmingham and Dudley (via Oldbury). Tel: 0871 200 2233.
TRAINS - half-hourly services to/from Birmingham Snow Hill and southwards towards Stourbridge, Kidderminster and Worcester. Tel: 03457 484950.
TAXIS - Premier Cars. Tel: 0121 552 7070.

Smethwick   Map 10

High Street was sliced in half to make room for the expressway. What remains is more Asian than Anglo-Saxon, but all the more intriguing for that. If you enjoy Asian cooking then this is the place to stop for authentic ingredients; the sweet shops are mouthwatering.

Eating & Drinking

SOHO FOUNDRY TAVERN - Foundry Lane. Tel: 0121 558 4670. Back street local which must have slaked the thirst of generations of foundrymen. Blend in with a pint of mild; food from 8am-2pm. B66 2LL

Things to Do

GALTON VALLEY CANAL MUSEUM - Brasshouse Lane. Tel: 0121 556 0683. Enjoyably interpreted canal history in authentic pumphouse setting. Open selected Saturdays 10am-3.30pm. B66 1BA

Connections

TRAINS - frequent services between Rolfe Street station and Birmingham New Street and between Galton Bridge and New Street and Snow Hill. Tel: 03457 484950

REALISATION of the impact made by Thomas Telford's new main line comes with exploration of the lengthy loops it super-seded. By the end of the 18th century Brindley's canal had become a victim of its own success; water was short and traffic congested. Telford was called in to suggest improvements and discovered 'a canal little better than a crooked ditch'! The original towing path had deteriorated to the extent that horses frequently slid and staggered into the water, tow lines entangled when boats met, and boatmen quarrelled over precedence at locks. The canny Scot devised a bold improvement plan cutting through the Smethwick summit. The work took five years and was completed in 1829. It reduced the distance between Wolverhampton and Birmingham by a third. A contemporary onlooker found the new route "unsurpassed in stupendous magnificence"!

It is difficult to this day not to be impressed by the puissance of Telford's engineering; though just as easy to be beguiled by Brindley's peregrinations. The old loops retained their local traffics, serving works firmly established along their banks. And so the Oozells Street, Icknield Port and Soho (though not the Cape nor Soho Foundry) loops remain navigable to this day, functioning - as does a greater part of the BCN - as storm drainage channels and linear reservoirs for industry. Included in the itineraries of Birmingham's trip boats, they are worth investigating as discursive alternatives

to the unequivocal, focussed concentration of the new main line.

Westwards from Smethwick Junction the old and new main lines forge their separate routes to and from Tipton. The earlier canal ascends through three locks (requiring 'handcuff' keys) to reach its 473ft summit. Originally its course lay even higher at 491ft, traces of which can be discerned along the embankment above the canal as it proceeds west of Brasshouse Lane Bridge. The Birmingham artist, Edward Richard Taylor, painted this view in all its unsullied glory in 1905: Galton Bridge shimmers in the distance whilst a horsedrawn narrowboat makes its way along the Old Line. The painting can be seen at Wednesbury Museum & Art Gallery. Nowadays a panoramic view in the opposite direction can be obtained from the footbridge straddling the railway. One cannot help but mourn, however, the disappearance of the Brasshouse Lane Foundry (and particularly the Sikhs amongst its labour force who would habitually cool off in the canal), transformed into housing marred by a sequence of descending terraces which would *continued overleaf:*

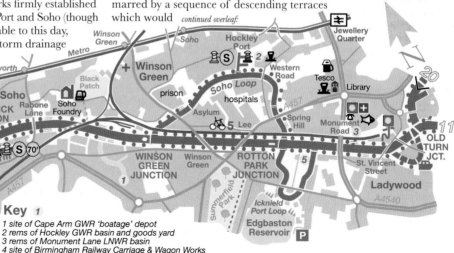

Key 1
1 site of Cape Arm GWR 'boatage' depot
2 rems of Hockley GWR basin and goods yard
3 rems of Monument Lane LNWR basin
4 site of Birmingham Railway Carriage & Wagon Works
5 site of Bellis & Morcom engineering works

*3 locks and an extra hour via
Old Main Line route

continued from page 29:

be more at home at West Bromwich Albion's nearby Hawthorns football ground.

Access to the celebrated Engine Arm is through the tiny arch of a stone side bridge adjacent to Smethwick Top Lock. The arm spans the new main line by way of a wonderfully Gothic iron bridge, a real treasure in the context of its industrial setting. Boating is busier on the arm since the provision of moorings, boating facilities and, most pertinently, a winding hole at its far end. The arm was built to serve as a feeder from Edgbaston Reservoir at Ladywood, and if you scale the grassy bank opposite the junction with the Soho Loop at Winson Green you can see the remnants of its narrow brick channel. The Engine Arm derives its name from James Watt's 'Smethwick Engine' of 1779 which was introduced to pump water up the original flight of six locks. Even when three of these were by-passed in 1790 the engine continued its work for another century until the pumping engine at Brasshouse Lane was commissioned. The 1892 pump house has become a distinctly more appropriate venue for the Galton Valley Canal Museum than the former pub which previously hosted it. West of here the old main line, running along the course engineered by Smeaton (of lighthouse fame) penetrates an unexpected oasis of water plantain and rosebay willowherb. For a moment it is possible to make believe you are deep in the countryside, but any rural illusion is shattered by the so-called Summit Tunnel, an ugly concrete tube covered by the high embankment of a dual carriageway.

Beyond the tunnel the canal is embraced by a deep and swarthy cutting and overlooked by the high rises of West Bromwich. The railway line into Snow Hill crosses the canal adjacent to the site of coal loading apparatus regrettably demolished on the grounds that it might collapse and pose a threat to public safety: the BCN equivalent of WMD. A totemic concrete structure, it had once been used to load boats with coal brought down by cable tramway from the Jubilee Colliery in Sandwell, and its removal broke yet another tenuous link with the BCN's working past.

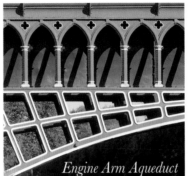

Engine Arm Aqueduct

A regular run from here was to King's Norton (Map 12) with coal for the furnaces of the paper mill.

In contrast with the old line's excursions over the summit, Telford's route lies in shadows cast by extensive earthworks; dank corridors of blue engineering brick retaining walls and precipitous banks of bracken and bramble. The scale of these 19th century works, accomplished by navvies totally without sophisticated machinery, can be overwhelming. But the climax is Telford's astonishing Galton Bridge; hidden in both directions by other structures until the last dramatic moment, and done no favours by rampant vegetation: it behoves the powers that be to consider the importance of sight-lines amidst their perennial initiative packages.

Between Smethwick and Winson Green the old and new main lines are one, sharing the same route through an industrial heartland of foundries and railway sidings. Much of the fun to be had from exploring the BCN derives from piecing together clues to its past. Railway boats would ease out of the Cape Arm's tunnel-like exit with nuts and bolts from GKN destined for the railway basin at Hockley Port; now a centre for residential moorings. Earlier still, near Rabone Lane Bridge, Matthew Boulton and James Watt opened their Soho foundry, the first factory in the world to be lit by gas so that work could continue after darkness had fallen. Visited by Boswell in 1776, Boulton boasted: 'I sell here, sir, what all the world desires to have - power!' Much of the Soho site remains in use by the weighing machine manufacturers, Avery. Nearby lies a parcel of common land known as the Black Patch. Implausible as it might seem, evidence has recently emerged to suggest that Charlie Chaplin was born in a gypsy camp on this site in 1889.

Adjacent to the western junction of the Soho Loop (and again beneath the Engine Arm aqueduct) stand the bases of former toll houses and gauging stops. A replica toll house has been erected alongside Smethwick Top Lock; though, regrettably, it seems to attract more attention from vandals than students of canal history.

O LD TURN JUNCTION might well be described as the pivotal point of the inland waterways network. Overlooked by the Barclaycard Arena and Sea Life Centre, it symbolises the massive changes which have overtaken the canals generally - and those of Birmingham and the Black Country in particular - during the last decade or two. All a far cry from the day, over two centuries ago, when a certain Mr Farmer's land was bisected by the new fangled waterway, and an accommodation bridge (long since demolished) erected to preserve his right of way. They rang the church bells all day when the canal reached Birmingham, and wild celebrations continued well into the night. The first section, completed in 1769, linked Birmingham with the mines at Wednesbury, and the price of coal is said to have halved. Interesting to reflect, then, that when the M40 motorway was extended from Oxford to the outskirts of Birmingham in 1990, no church bells rang with glee and no prices fell in the department stores of Corporation Street. During the rest of the 18th Century, Birmingham became a magnet for canal promoters and, in 1794, the Birmingham Canal Navigations were formed, amounting to some 160 miles of waterway, of which 100 miles remain navigable in an area bounded by Wolverhampton, Walsall, Dudley and Tamworth.

There *were* celebrations, however, in 1991 when the Convention Centre opened alongside the canal, and Birmingham, here, has something to be proud of. Delegates from all over the world are wooed to convene in Birmingham instead of Brussels or Baltimore, and who knows what indelible magic of the BCN might rub off on them.

Brindley Place lies at the centre of things now. Here are 24 hour moorings overlooked by a plethora of cafe bars and restaurants - for once the hackneyed analogy of Birmingham with Venice seems almost understated, even disingenuous, and you cannot help but think that of all the British cities to see virtue in revitalizing their canals, Birmingham has made the best fist of it. From the piazzas of the Convention Centre the canal leads through Broad Street tunnel to Gas Street Basin, the epitome - though for some the lost soul - of Birmingham's waterways.

In fact Gas Street had come to symbolise the BCN to such an extent that it was often forgotten that the actual terminal wharf and offices of the Birmingham Canal lay to the east of here. Two arms terminated at the rear of the BCN company's handsomely symmetrical offices on Suffolk Street which, sadly, were demolished in 1928. Demolition

continued overleaf:

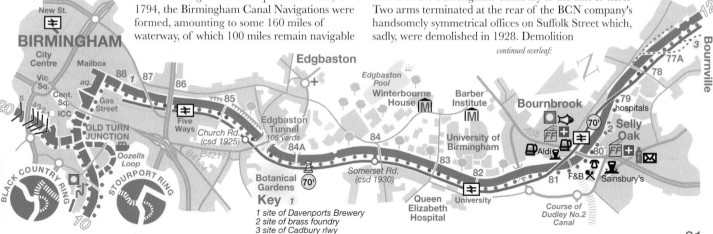

Key 1
1 site of Davenports Brewery
2 site of brass foundry
3 site of Cadbury rlwy

continued from page 31

controversially took its toll of the Gas Street canalscape in 1975 as well, by which time the planners should have known better, and British Waterways were never really forgiven for razing their rich heritage of 18th century waterside warehouses to the ground in a calculated move to sidestep a preservation order.

For a time nothing was done to fill the void. Gas Street might have ceased to exist but for a community of residential boats which lent a splash of colour and humanity to a decaying canalscape. A decade elapsed before the developer's proposals were realised in bricks and mortar, and the biggest irony of all is that the new pubs and offices emerged in a warehouse vernacular style of remarkable similarity to the bulldozed originals. The only post Seventies interloper unsympathetic to the scale of the original Gas Street is the towering, shimmering, slippery, silvered edifice of the Hyatt Hotel. What do its sybaritic guests make of the little boats miles below their air-conditioned eyries? Do they see them as 'local colour', as archaic as the sampans of Hong Kong harbour?

The Worcester & Birmingham Canal

Work began on the Worcester & Birmingham Canal from the Birmingham end in 1794, but it was not until 1815 that the route was completed throughout. Fearful of its water supply disappearing down into the Severn, the Birmingham Canal Company at first refused to be directly linked with the newcomer, and so laborious transhipment of through traffic took place across an infamous divide known as the 'Worcester Bar'. Eventually, however, a stop lock was provided between the two waterways, affording the BCN some measure of protection, yet enabling through passage of boats.

Quickly extricating itself from the wine bars and nightclubs of downtown Birmingham, the Worcester & Birmingham Canal turns right-angle past The Mailbox development - together with its lofty neighbour, The Cube - and makes for the sylvan suburbs of Edgbaston. It was this cloistered, arboreous entrance to and exit from the city that prompted Robert Aickman to express the aphorism: "Canals stretch green fingers into towns." We can't help but share his enthusiasm, for this is a lovely stretch of canal - given its proximity to the city centre - and its towpath is increasingly used by walkers and cyclists as an alternative to the choked and inherently lethal carriageways of the A38.

In cahoots with the old Birmingham West Suburban Railway, opened in 1876, and now heavily nose to tail with suburban and inter-city trains, the canal skirts the purlieus of Birmingham University, whose Italianate tower 'Uncle Joe' stabs the sky.

At Selly Oak there are plans - unrealised as yet - for part of the former Dudley No.2 Canal to be re-opened in conjunction with a retail development scheme led by Sainsbury's. Journeying southwards, the Worcester & Birmingham reaches the outskirts of the chocolate making centre of Bournville. Again there are scant remains of the canal's heyday, when its east bank was a busy point of interchange for Cadbury's fleet of narrowboats and its internal railway system shunted by its own fleet of perky tank locomotives painted in a dark red colour inspired by the company's cocoa tins.

Away2service's mobile 'service boat' operates in the vicinity of Old Turn Junction providing pump-out, fuel, gas, coal and repairs & servicing facilities. Tel: 0845 644 5344

Birmingham
Maps 11 & 20

Canal boating holidays come low enough in the kudos stakes, and Birmingham as a destination lower still. But any sympathy your friends can muster will be wasted. Let them bake on some beach. There is more character in Birmingham's big toe than the whole of 'The Med' put together. The city centre is only a brief stroll from the visitor moorings radiating from Old Turn Junction, and its sophisticated character and traffic-free thoroughfares may surprise those with preconceived notions of an ungainly, uncouth city where everyone speaks through their nose and has something to do with the motor trade. But cars have lost their pole position in 'Brummagem's' scheme of things and the city continues to recover from its crass submission to traffic which ruined it a generation ago. Centenary, Chamberlain (being redeveloped) and Victoria squares set the tone for the canal travellers' perambulation of the city. The first revitalised with the opening of the Convention Centre in 1991, the other two dominated by imposing Victoriana, including the Art Gallery and the Town Hall. There are deeper oases of calm and character to be discovered too. Churches like St Philip's Cathedral and St Paul's (the 'Jeweller's Church'), the bustling markets of the rebuilt Bull Ring, and the quiet backwaters of the Jewellery Quarter. These are the bits of Birmingham you should make it your business to see and appreciate.

Eating & Drinking
BANK - Brindley Place. Tel: 0121 633 4466. Stylish restaurant overlooking the Oozells Loop. B1 2JP
CARLUCCIO'S - Brindley Place. Tel: 0121 633 9262. Italian cafe/restaurant/deli. B1 2HP
COTE - The Mailbox. Tel: 0121 631 1587. Canalside Parisian style brasserie. B1 1RX
FIDDLE & BONE - Sheepcote Street. Tel: 0121 200 2223. Bar/restaurant housed in buildings associated with characterful roundhouse stables. B16 8AE
MILLER & CARTER - The Mailbox. Tel: 0121 643 7738. High quality steaks for famished boaters. B1 1RN
THE WELLINGTON - Bennett's Hill. Tel: 0121 200 3115. *GBG* listed real ale venue between Colmore Row and New Street. Up to fifteen beers on tap. B2 5SN
VIVAANTA - Holliday Wharf (opp The Mailbox) at what used to be known as Salvage Turn. Tel: 0121 665 6568. Canalside Indian restaurant. B1 1SN

Shopping
Canallers in a hurry - if that's not a contradiction in terms - will find convenience stores adjoining the Mailbox, Oozells Loop and Tindal Bridge by Farmer's Bridge Junction. Otherwise you'll find all the facilities of a major city within easy reach of the canal. The Bull Ring markets (located on Edgbaston Street south-east of New Street station) are a famous focal point of midland merchandising. The Bull Ring Shopping Centre - a painful lesson in the excesses of concrete architecture from the Sixties - has been redeveloped, the landmark Rotunda having escaped by the skin of its Grade II listed teeth, so that it now rubs shoulders with the likes of Kaplicky's shimmering Selfridges store. Grand Central is the city's latest shopping experience located above its revitalised New Street railway station. Sophisticated fashion in The Mailbox.

Things to Do
COFFIN WORKS - Fleet Street. Tel: 0121 233 4790. Tours of Victorian factory embalmed in aspic. B3 1JP
CYCLE CHAIN - Central Sq. Brindley Place. Tel: 0754758 7050. Bicycle hire/repair from the 1935 Yardwoods butty *Carina*. B1 2HL
IKON GALLERY - Oozells Sq, Brindley Place. Tel: 0121 248 0708. Contemporary art venue. B1 2HS
LIBRARY OF BIRMINGHAM - Centenary Square. Tel: 0121 242 4242. From the Secret Garden on the 7th floor there are bird's eye views over the canals radiating from Old Turn Junction. B1 2ND
MUSEUM & ART GALLERY - Chamberlain Square. Tel: 0121 303 1966. Open daily, admission free. Rivals Manchester in the richness of its Pre-Raphaelite collection. Shop, Edwardian Tea Room. B3 3DH
MUSEUM OF THE JEWELLERY QUARTER - Vyse Street (Hockley). Open Mon-Sat. Quarter of an hour's walk from Farmer's Bridge but well signposted. Open Mon-Sat. Tel: 0121 554 3598. Housed in former jewellery factory. Shop & refreshments. B18 6HA
NATIONAL SEA LIFE CENTRE - Brindley Place. Tel: 0871 423 2110. Turtles, sharks and other non BCN resident maritime species. B1 2HL
PEN MUSEUM - Frederick Street. Tel: 0121 236 9834. Fascinating story of the writing pen trade. B1 3HS
SYMPHONY HALL - Broad Street. Tel: 0121 345 0600. Canalside concert hall. B1 2EA
THINKTANK - Curzon Street. Tel: 0121 348 8000. Science can be fun! Home to Watt's Smethwick Engine and Stanier's *City of Birmingham*. B4 7XG
WONDERFUL WORLD OF TRAINS & PLANES - St Paul's Sq. Tel: 0121 227 4000. B3 1BG

Connections
BUSES - Tel: 0871 200 2233.
TRAINS - Tel: 03457 484950.
METRO - Tel: 0871 200 2233.
TAXIS - TOA (black cabs). Tel: 0121 427 8888.

Edgbaston
Map 11

More than merely a leafy suburb and test cricket venue, Edgbaston rewards patient exploration beyond the Worcester & Birmingham Canal corridor.

Things to Do
BARBER INSTITUTE - University of Birmingham. Tel: 0121 414 7333. Art gallery of international repute (featuring works by Monet, Gainsborough, Van Gogh etc) open 10am - 5pm Mon-Sat and 12pm-5pm Sun. Admission free. B15 2TS
WINTERBOURNE HOUSE - Edgbaston. Tel: 0121 414 3003. Lovely Arts & Crafts house erected 1903 for the industrialist John Nettlefield of GKN fame. Gardens inspired by Gertrude Jekyll. Open from 10am daily. Shop and tea room. B15 2RT

COMMERCIAL activity on the canal is sadly no longer considered a viable proposition, but leisure boating does bring its fair share of visitors to Cadbury World. Access from the offside visitor moorings is westwards along Bournville Lane which runs beneath the canal. Eastwards, you'll come upon two handsome rows of former shops labelled 'Bournville Markets' and Stirchley's imposing swimming baths, recently reborn (without the water) as a community hub.

Bournville's garden village owes its existence to the altruism of Quakers Richard and George Cadbury, who built a chocolate factory on a greenfield site in the vicinity in 1879. It was George in particular who had visions of a worker's paradise, commissioning the architect Alexander Harvey to design artisans' dwellings on a 120 acre site. Each house was to have a garden with fruit trees and a vegetable patch to provide an element of self-sufficiency - one cannot live on chocolate alone.

Between bridges 75 and 73 the towpath swaps sides, not on a whim, but because the Midland Railway once operated a transhipment basin on the west bank of the canal.

At King's Norton the Stratford Canal comes in to join the Worcester & Birmingham, a route described in the *South Midlands* and *Severn & Avon Canal Companions*. A sizeable paper mill formerly overlooked the canal junction and large quantities of coal were brought here by narrowboat from Black Country mines. The old Junction House is backed by the soaring steeple of St Nicholas, the parish church of King's Norton, where the Rev W. Awdry of *Thomas the Tank Engine* fame was a curate during the Second World War.

At 2,726 yards, Wast Hill Tunnel is the Worcester & Birmingham's longest. It takes around half an hour to pass through and, whilst appearances can be deceptive, rest assured that there *is* room to pass oncoming craft inside its gloomy depths. Like all Worcester & Birmingham tunnels (except Edgbaston), it has no towpath. The lads who led their boat

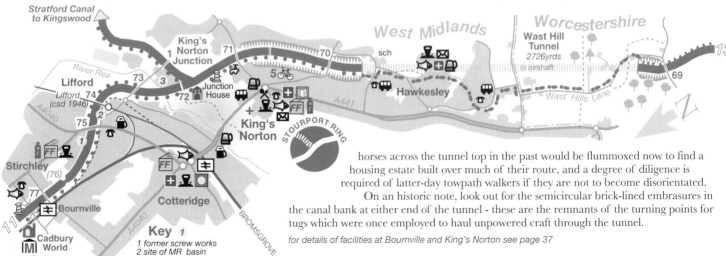

horses across the tunnel top in the past would be flummoxed now to find a housing estate built over much of their route, and a degree of diligence is required of latter-day towpath walkers if they are not to become disorientated.

On an historic note, look out for the semicircular brick-lined embrasures in the canal bank at either end of the tunnel - these are the remnants of the turning points for tugs which were once employed to haul unpowered craft through the tunnel.

for details of facilities at Bournville and King's Norton see page 37

Key 1
1 former screw works
2 site of MR basin
3 former paper mill

13 WORCESTER & BIRMINGHAM CANAL Alvechurch 5mls/0lks/2hrs

POST-WAR Alvechurch overspills up its hillside to impinge upon the canal, but barely deflects from its dreamy, lockless progress above the valley of the River Arrow. There are panoramic views eastwards towards Weatheroak Hill crossed by the Roman's Ryknild Street. A feeder comes in from Upper Bittell Reservoir beside an isolated canal employee's cottage near Bridge 66. The Lower Reservoir, rich in wildfowl, lies alongside the canal and is given a gorgeous wooded backdrop by the Lickey Hills. Only the Upper Reservoir feeds the canal, the Lower was provided to compensate millers whose water supplies from the Arrow had been detrimentally affected by construction of the canal. A short section of the canal was re-routed in 1985 to accommodate construction of the M42 motorway.

Bridge 62 carries the electrified commuter line from Redditch through Birmingham to Lichfield. A seventy-five minute train journey ... three days by boat to the nearest canal settlement at Fradley Junction. But time is an irrelevance on the canals, so relax and savour the charms of Shortwood Tunnel, its approach cuttings so suffocated by the odour of wild garlic that you feel as if you are being embraced by an over enthusiastic Frenchman. All that's missing is the tang of Gauloise, but then you may be able to provide that (and/or the Frenchman) yourself.

As with all other Worcester & Birmingham tunnels (Edgbaston excepted) the towpath isn't subterranean, but the old horse-path across the top remains well-defined, and it is pleasant to wander across the top, fantasising that you've a horse to lead while your boat is hauled through the earth beneath your feet by one of the erstwhile tunnel tugs as described so evocatively by Tom Foxon in his book *Number One*.

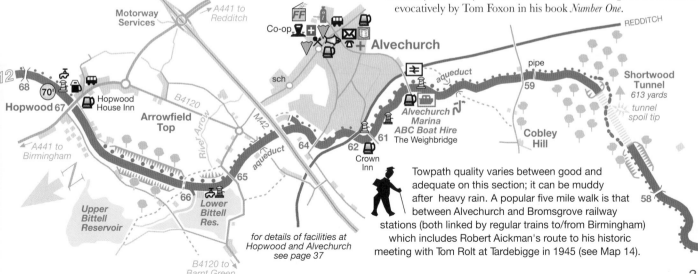

Towpath quality varies between good and adequate on this section; it can be muddy after heavy rain. A popular five mile walk is that between Alvechurch and Bromsgrove railway stations (both linked by regular trains to/from Birmingham) which includes Robert Aickman's route to his historic meeting with Tom Rolt at Tardebigge in 1945 (see Map 14).

for details of facilities at Hopwood and Alvechurch see page 37

TARDEBIGGE represents a boater's Rite of Passage. Once you have tackled this flight which, coupled with the neighbouring six at Stoke, amount to thirty-six locks in four miles, other groups of locks, however fiendish, however formidable, pale into insignificance. The thirty chambers of the Tardebigge flight raise the canal over two hundred feet, the top lock - somewhat removed from the rest - being, at 14 feet, one of the deepest narrowbeam locks on the system; it replaced a lift dysfunctionally prone to recalcitrance and water wastage. Well maintained and surrounded by fine countryside, with wonderful views to the Malvern Hills, Tardebigge Locks are there to be enjoyed, not dreaded. And in the summer months you'll have plenty of fellow travellers with

direct result of their meeting the Inland Waterways Association was formed. A plinth adjacent to the lock tells the story, along with a supplementary plaque correcting the date to 1945 - as Pearsons had immodestly and intuitively affirmed all along!

Only the briefest of pounds separates the Tardebigge and Stoke flights. Room enough, just, for half a dozen boats to moor for an overnight breather. The picturesque lock-keeper's cottage between locks 31 and 32 is available for holiday lets from the Landmark Trust, a body devoted to the rescue and refurbishment of worthwhile buildings in all shapes and sizes. A wheelbarrow is at the disposal of guests for the conveyance of luggage along the towpath. It was the demolition of the junction house at Hurleston, on the Shropshire Union Canal, which 'maddened' the Trust's founder, John Smith, into creating this laudable organisation in 1965.

whom to share the experience, never mind the work. Tardebigge's 18th century church, with its slender 135ft spire, is an inspirational landmark: 'belatedly baroque' in the words of James Lees-Milne in his pithy 1964 *Shell Guide to Worcestershire*. Another spire to look out for - on the western horizon - is that of Bromsgrove's parish church, St John the Baptist.

Tardebigge holds a special place in the story of the inland waterways movement. It was to here that Robert Aickman and his wife made their way from Bromsgrove railway station to meet Tom and Angela Rolt aboard their narrowboat home *Cressy* which had been moored above the top lock throughout the Second World War. As a

Bournville
Map 12

Use of a CART 'facilities' key provides access from the secure offside moorings opposite Bournville railway station to the enchanting 'garden village' of Bournville and its arboreal street nomenclature.

Things to Do
CADBURY WORLD - Linden Road. Tel: 0844 880 7667. 'A whole world of chocolatey fun!' B30 2LU
SELLY MANOR - Maple Road. Tel: 0121 472 0199. Five minutes and five hundred years away from all that 'chocolatey fun'. B30 2AE

King's Norton
Map 12

Arguably the most easily accessible facilities for canal travellers in this area. 48 hour moorings are provided between bridges 71 and 72 and it's only a short uphill walk to the centre, grouped about a pretty green and overlooked by the imposing spire of St Nicholas' Church. Queen Henrietta Maria stopped here overnight on her way to meet Charles I at Edge Hill. Half-timbered 17th century grammar school in churchyard.

Shopping
Facilities include: a pharmacy, Spar shop, post office, newsagent, off licence, and Lloyds bank.

Eating & Drinking
MOLLY'S - The Green. Tel: 0121 459 9500. Cheerful cafe, good for breakfasts. B38 8SD

Things to Do
ST NICHOLAS PLACE - Tel: 0121 458 1223. Heritage Centre adjoining church. Tours Fri & Sat. B38 8RU

Hopwood
Map 13

HOPWOOD HOUSE INN - canalside Bridge 67. Tel: 0121 445 1716. Comfortably furnished Marston's 'Rotisserie' pub/restaurant open from noon. B48 7AB. *Petrol station with convenience store to south of Bridge 67. Small garden centre nearby. Buses to/from Birmingham.*

Alvechurch
Map 13

It's one thing strolling down from the canal, but an altogether different matter struggling back with shopping bags. Nevertheless, Alvechurch is a pleasant Worcestershire village with some worthwhile facilities.

Eating & Drinking
THE WEIGHBRIDGE - canalside Bridge 60. Tel: 0121 445 5111. The 'weighbridge house' for a coal wharf in days gone by. Tillerman's Tipple is brewed for them by Weatheroak. Home cooked food lunchtimes and evenings (ex Tue & Wed); breakfasts by prior arrangement. B48 7SQ
THE CROWN - canalside Bridge 61. Tel: 0121 445 2300. An unspoilt canalside pub. B48 7PN
There is also a Chinese takeaway (Tel: 0121 447 8085) and an Indian restaurant (Tel: 0121 445 5583).

Shopping
Co-op, post office (with newspapers) pharmacy, two butchers, off-licence, greengrocer and florist.

Connections
TRAINS - half-hourly service to Redditch and Birmingham. Tel: 03457 484950.

Aston Fields
Map 14

Aston Fields, a suburb of Bromsgrove, has a number of shops - notably BANNERS deli and hot food outlet established as long ago as 1906 (Tel: 01527 872581 - B60 2DZ) and now they have opened an excellent cafe/restaurant as well (Tel: 01527 872889) open from 8am daily and providing evening meals Wed-Sat. Bromsgrove's railway station is here too, for taxis telephone Gold & Black on 01527 570707.

Stoke Wharf
Map 14

A pair of stylishly refurbished pubs vie for your custom and offer just reward for the effort involved in working all those locks: QUEEN'S HEAD by Bridge 48 (Tel: 01527 557007 - B60 3AU) and the NAVIGATION by Bridge 44 (Tel: 01527 831600 - B60 4LB) where PRIORY CAFE (Tel: 01527 880660 - B60 4JZ) also provides eat in/take-away food Mon-Fri 6am-3pm, Sat 8am-12pm. AVONCROFT MUSEUM, a mile north of Bridge 48, houses a wonderful collection of buildings saved from demolition (Tel: 01527 831363 - B60 4JR).

Stoke Works
Map 15

The BOAT & RAILWAY (Tel: 01527 831065 - B60 4EQ) is a Marston's/Banks's pub with a nice canalside terrace, good choice of beers and a wide range of bar meals (not Sundays) and a skittle alley. Take-away food is also available. The Worcester & Birmingham Canal Society regularly meet here.

Hanbury Wharf
Map 15

At Hanbury Wharf the EAGLE & SUN (Tel: 01905 799266 - WR9 7DX) is a steak bar and carvery.

Dunhampstead
Map 16

The quiet hamlet of Dunhampstead is able to offer both a canalside craft shop (Forge Crafts) and a well-appointed pub called THE FIR TREE INN (Tel: 01905 774094 - WR9 7JX) which serves tasty food and Hook Norton within its designer interior.

Tibberton
Map 16

Many villages of this size can no longer muster a single pub, Tibberton manages two. The post office stores provide stamps, provender and gossip in equal measure, whilst postcards and prints by the local wildlife artist, John Horton, are on sale. Of the pubs, the BRIDGE INN (Tel: 01905 345874 - WR9 7NQ) is the more canal orientated, having a large waterside garden and offering a good choice of food; however the SPEED THE PLOUGH (Tel: 01905 345146 - WR9 7NQ) can equally be recommended. Buses connect the village with Worcester - Tel: 0871 200 2233.

15 WORCESTER & BIRMINGHAM CANAL Hanbury 4mls/6lks/2.5hrs

NOWADAYS, Britain's salt industry is largely confined to Cheshire but, as the name Droitwich suggests, this part of Worcestershire was once a centre of salt making too. The salt obsessed Romans built a special road between Droitwich and Alcester to carry this valuable commodity. Similarly, the Worcester & Birmingham built the short Droitwich Junction Canal from Hanbury Wharf to carry the same cargo. Abandoned in 1939, it has become one of the success stories of the canal restoration movement, finally re-opening in 2011 and forming, along with the Droitwich Barge Canal (see Map 18) what will undoubtedly become a hugely popular circular route - the Mid-Worcestershire Ring. Full coverage will be found in *Pearson's Severn & Avon Canal & River Companion*. If you're remaining loyal to the W& B's 'main line', it would be churlish not at least to stroll down the first three locks as far as Gateway Park, offering votive thanks as you go to those who steadfastly kept the faith with regard to the canal's second coming.

At the end of the 18th century, John Corbett, son of a local boatman, discovered large deposits of brine at Stoke Prior and developed one of the largest saltworks in the world on the site. It made his fortune. He met an Irish woman in Paris, married her and erected a replica French chateau for her on the outskirts of Droitwich, a town he transformed from one of industrial squalor into a fashionable spa. In its heyday the canalside works at Stoke was producing 200,000 tons of salt a year. The company had a fleet of fifty narrowboats and hundreds of railway wagons. Corbett died in 1901 and is buried at the pretty little church of St Michael's, Stoke Prior (Map 14). The 'John Corbett Way', a seven and a half mile waymarked trail, has been developed between Stoke Heath and Droitwich.

Attractive countryside returns at Astwood Locks, as canal and railway drift lazily through lush farmland overlooked by the wooded slopes of Summer Hill to the east. Westward views encompass Abberley and Woodbury hills beyond the River Severn. Closer at hand are the twin 700ft high masts of Wychbold radio transmitting station. Opened in 1934, its call sign "Droitwich Calling" became known throughout Britain and in many parts of Europe. During the Second World War Droitwich's long range transmitter broadcast the 'voice of freedom' throughout occupied Europe.

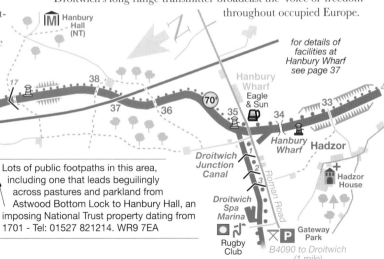

for details of facilities at Hanbury Wharf see page 37

Hanbury Hall (NT)

Hanbury Wharf

Eagle & Sun

Droitwich Junction Canal

Hanbury Wharf

Hadzor

Hadzor House

Roman Road

site of salt works

social club

Boat & Railway

Stoke Works (csd 1966)

Stoke Works

for details of facilities at Stoke Works see page 37

Bowling Green

Astwood Locks 17-22 42ft 0ins

Wychbold

Lots of public footpaths in this area, including one that leads beguilingly across pastures and parkland from Astwood Bottom Lock to Hanbury Hall, an imposing National Trust property dating from 1701 - Tel: 01527 821214. WR9 7EA

Droitwich Spa Marina

Rugby Club

Gateway Park

B4090 to Droitwich (1 mile)

16 WORCESTER & BIRMINGHAM CANAL Oddingley 4mls/6lks/2hrs

THE canal skirts the mellow settlements of Shernal Green, Dunhampstead, Oddingley and Tibberton and, in spite of being sandwiched by the railway and motorway, seems remote and untouched. High clumps of sedge border the canal, swaying with the passage of each boat and somehow emphasising the loneliness of the landscape. At Shernal Green the Wychavon Way - a 42-mile long distance footpath running from Holt Fleet on the River Severn to Winchcombe in Gloucestershire - makes its way over the canal.

Dunhampstead Tunnel is tiny compared to the 'big three' to the north, but like them it has no towpath, forcing walkers to take to the old horse-path through deciduous woodlands above. A hire base adds traffic to the canal at this point, whilst a craft shop and convivial country pub provide an excuse to break your journey.

Oddingley consists of little more than an ancient manor house, a tiny church and a level-crossing keeper's cabin of typical Midland Railway style. Murder was done here in 1806! Visit the Fir Tree Inn for further details.

Tibberton is a long straggling village of mostly modern housing. Well piled visitor moorings are provided west of Bridge 25.

A deep cutting and the M5 motorway

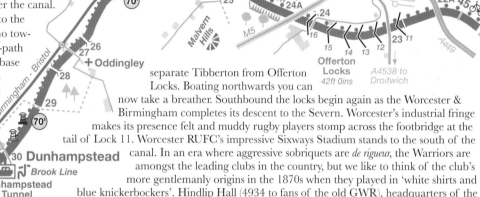

separate Tibberton from Offerton Locks. Boating northwards you can now take a breather. Southbound the locks begin again as the Worcester & Birmingham completes its descent to the Severn. Worcester's industrial fringe makes its presence felt and muddy rugby players stomp across the footbridge at the tail of Lock 11. Worcester RUFC's impressive Sixways Stadium stands to the south of the canal. In an era where aggressive sobriquets are *de rigueur*, the Warriors are amongst the leading clubs in the country, but we like to think of the club's more gentlemanly origins in the 1870s when they played in 'white shirts and blue knickerbockers'. Hindlip Hall (4934 to fans of the old GWR), headquarters of the County Constabulary and refuge, in its original Elizabethan guise, of two members of the Gunpowder Plot, dominates the hillside to the north-west.

Two aspects of this canal's working practice were remarkable. Boats kept *left* when passing each other and pairs of donkeys were widely used in place of horses to haul the boats. The animals worked well together as long as they 'knew' one another, but the introduction of a new donkey would cause considerable ructions. One of the last traders on the Worcester & Birmingham Canal was Charles Ballinger of Gloucester. He was still using horse-drawn boats as late as 1954, carrying coal from the Cannock area to Townsend's mill at Diglis. Occasionally he would have an 'uphill' cargo as well: matches from Gloucester to Birmingham, or flour from Worcester to Tipton; but by the beginning of the Sixties trade had deserted the canal.

for details of facilities at Dunhampstead and Tibberton see page 37

WATERSIDE Worcester has always enjoyed a flagrant love affair with the Severn, but in modern times the canal has come into its own. From Tolladine down, the towpath is popular with pedestrians and cyclists alike. Burgeoning industrial estates accompany the canal but do little to spoil it. Cadbury's once had a busy wharf at Black Pole linked by water transport to their premises at Bournville and Frampton-on-Severn. A leisure centre and municipal golf course border the canal above Bilford Upper Lock. Worcester City sold their St George's Lane ground by Bridge 12 to property developers in 2013, and, after a period of playing their home games in Kidderminster have moved to Bromsgrove. North of Bridge 11 school playing fields are overlooked by an imposing pavilion.

A shapely railway bridge (10) spans the canal by Lowesmoor Wharf. It has a hole cut out of it, presumably to lessen the weight of the structure. Lowesmoor Wharf (aka Worcester Marina) is a good spot to moor securely close to the city centre - just slip beneath the roving bridge and ask permission at the office.

An Italianate clock tower peeps over the canal by Bridge 8, the former Engine Works of 1864. Known now as Shrub Hill Industrial Estate, within the confines of a corrugated-iron clad workshop, someone appears to be still archaically bashing-metal. In marked contrast, the premises of Pizza Hut overlook Bridge 5A. Locks at Blockhouse and Sidbury lower the canal towards the Severn. Between them, on the offside, Fownes Hotel was formerly a glove factory. Virtually opposite

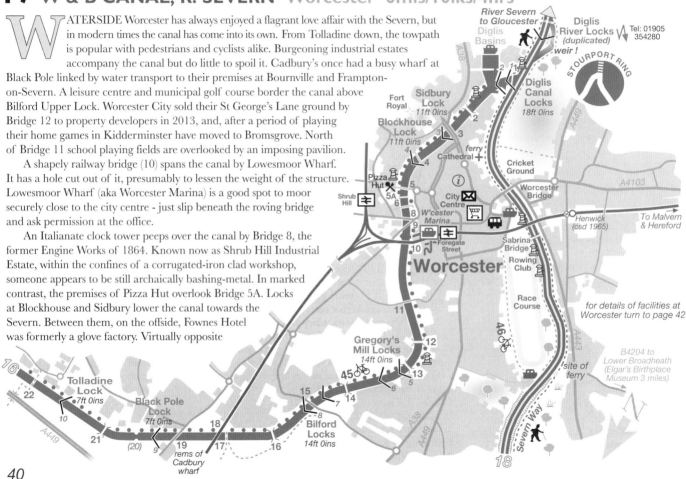

for details of facilities at
Worcester turn to page 42

stands The Commandery which Charles II used as his headquarters during the Civil War Battle of Worcester in 1651, though it was originally a hospital and dates from as early as the 15th century. There is space here for some half a dozen boats to moor overnight within euphonious earshot of the cathedral clock. Sidbury Lock lies near the site of a gate in the city wall where a thousand Royalist troops are said to have been killed. Cromwell's men had captured the nearby fort and turned its canons on the escaping Cavaliers. The elevated fort is a pleasant park now, easily reached from the Commandery moorings. A panoramic plaque identifies major incidents of the Battle of Worcester and the gardens offer a marvellous view over the city. Bridge 3 carries amusing sculptures of Civil War pikestaffs, shields and helmets.

Burgeoning apartment blocks usher the canal down to Diglis. Townsend's Mill (by Bridge 2) once an intensive user of water transport, has been incorporated in these developments. Royal Worcester's porcelain works has not been so fortunate, and is gradually being redeveloped. Nowadays, what's left of the ceramic 'brand' is manufactured in either Stoke-on-Trent or Bangladesh!

Diglis Basins opened in the 19th century to facilitate transhipment of cargoes between river and canal. One would have relished being here in their working heyday. Rebranded now as Diglis Water, they offer - to the amazement and incomprehension, one imagines, of the spirits of boatmen and dock workers who presumably haunt the place - 'a whole new environment for living and working in the modern world'.

Two broad locks separate the basins from the river. They are closed

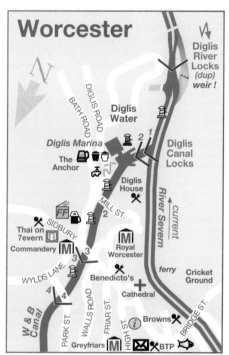

overnight, re-opening at eight in the morning. Entering or leaving the river can pose problems, especially if the current is flowing quickly, and getting your crew on or off for the locks needs careful consideration. One of the easiest access points is the pontoon immediately downstream of the lock entrance.

Downstream the river heads for Tewkesbury and Gloucester through Diglis River Locks as covered in our *Severn & Avon Canal Companion*. Upstream, 'Sabrina' flows beneath the great west window of the Cathedral, the juxtaposition of the noble building and the wide river being one of the great inland waterway scenes. A recent addition is King's School's striking, prow-shaped boathouse. On summer weekends a ferry operates in the vicinity of the Cathedral, and trip boats ply this reach as well, so keep a weather eye open for sudden manoeuvres. Antiquated wharves and warehouses line the east bank of the river south of Worcester Bridge. Widened in the 1930s, the old parapet found its way into Edward Elgar's garden, so enamoured was the composer of anything associated with his home town. Limited official moorings are available on the city side between the old road bridge and the ornate, cast iron railway bridge which carries the pretty Malvern and Hereford line across the river. A third bridge spanning the Severn is of modern origin, being a stylish pedestrian link (much used by students) between the city centre and the west bank suburbs: the Severn Way swaps sides at this point. Passing rowing clubs, the racecourse, and some enviable riverside properties - some of which would not look out of place beside the Thames - the river traveller heads upstream for more rural locales.

Worcester
Map 17

Descending from Birmingham to Worcester, the West Midlands are left intuitively behind, and you find yourself in streets where the patois has a distinct West Country burr - when it s not eastern European, that is. Royal Worcester suffered more than most at the hands of the developers during the philistine Sixties (Ian Nairn, the late architectural writer and broadcaster, was incensed, and James Lees-Milne got into hot water for permitting his *Shell Guide to Worcestershire* to be too critical) but much making of amends has been done in recent years to enhance the city's fabric. The Cathedral, gazing devoutly over the Severn and containing the tomb of King John shares, with Gloucester and Hereford, Europe's oldest music festival, 'The Three Choirs'. From the deep well of Worcester's history you can draw inspiration from almost any era that captures your imagination. This was the 'faithful city' of the Civil War from which Charles II escaped following the final defeat of the Cavaliers. It was the home, for much of his life, of Sir Edward Elgar. Home too of that ensign of the empire, Lea & Perrins sauce; though they have recently lost their independence to Heinz. And here you'll find one of the country's loveliest cricketing venues, Worcestershire's New Road ground.

Eating & Drinking
THE ANCHOR - Diglis. Tel: 01905 351094. Marston s local alongside Diglis Basins. Breakfasts from 9.30am. Skittle alley and canalside patio. WR5 3BW
BENEDICTO S - Sidbury. Tel: 01905 21444. Italian on the Cathedral side of Sidbury Lock. WR1 2HZ
BOSTON TEA PARTY - Broad Street. Tel: 01905 26472. Part of a growing chain (Barnstaple, Bath, Bristol, Birmingham etc) this charming cafe opens daily 7.30am (9am Suns) offering a wide range of food and drinks all carefully (and mostly locally) sourced. WR1 3NF

BROWNS AT THE QUAY - Quay Street. Tel: 01905 21800. Stylish restaurant housed in former riverside mill (closed Mons). WR1 2JN
DIGLIS HOUSE HOTEL - Riverside. Tel: 01905 353518. Best to moor in basins and walk back for good bar and restaurant meals; nice views over the Severn towards the cricket ground. WR1 2NF
THAI ON 7EVERN - Sidbury. Tel: 01905 769054. Thai restaurant handy for moorings either side of Bridge 3 - turn left on reaching pavement. WR1 2HU

Shopping
The Shambles, Friar Street and New Street feature numerous fascinating little shops and small businesses. Crown Gate is the main shopping precinct with adjoining street markets on Tue-Sat. A new Asda supermarket in the St Martin s Quarter on Lowesmoor is easily accessible from bridges 8/9 and/or Worcester Marina. Also handy on Lowesmoor are convenience stores, a butcher, launderette and fish & chips.

Things to Do
TOURIST INFORMATION CENTRE - The Guildhall, High Street. Tel: 01905 726311. WR1 2EY
THE COMMANDERY - canalside by Sidbury Lock. Tel: 01905 361821. Civil War history museum. WR1 2HU
CITY MUSEUM & ART GALLERY - Foregate Street. Tel: 01902 25371. Admission free. One or two works by Benjamin Williams Leader (brother of the canal engineer Edward Leader Williams) perhaps best known for February Fill Dyke which hangs in Birmingham Art Gallery if you re going that way. WR1 1DT
TUDOR HOUSE - Friar Street. Tel: 01905 612309. Local history displays in five hunded year old half-timbered house. Admission free. WR1 2NA
MUSEUM OF ROYAL WORCESTER - Severn Street. Tel: 01905 21247. Sadly, all that s left of the famous pottery, though items still for sale. WR1 2ND

Connections
TRAINS - stations at Foregate Street and Shrub Hill. Services to/from the Malverns (and on through the hopyards to Hereford) Droitwich, Kidderminster, Birmingham etc. Good service also to and from London Paddington via Oxford and the picturesque Cotswolds line. Tel: 03457 484950.
BUSES - links throughout the area, but Diamond services 294/5, which connect Worcester with Stourport every couple of hours Mon-Sat, facilitate walks along the Severn Way. Tel: 0871 200 2233.
TAXIS - Cathedral Cars. Tel: 01905 767400.

Bevere
Map 18

THE CAMP HOUSE - riverside downstream of Bevere Lock. Tel: 01905 640288. Peacocks in the garden, Bathams beer and rabbit pie render this isolated riverside inn a veritable heaven on earth. Limited moorings for customers. WR2 6LX

Holt Fleet
Map 19

Good place to stop on the Severn, a pontoon being provided between the tail of the lock and the bridge.

Eating & Drinking
THE HOLT FLEET - west bank. Tel: 01905 620286. Architecturally ostentatious Thirties road house, now a family-owned inn/restaurant. WR6 6NL
THE WHARF INN - east bank. Tel: 01905 620337. Food & accommodation. WR6 6NN
Other riverside pubs between Holt and Stourport include the Lenchford Inn (Tel: 01905 620229 - WR6 6TB) and the Hampstall Inn (Tel: 01299 822600 - DY13 0RY) which both offer customer moorings.

Shopping
Convenience store (gas, coal and logs) and recycling point. The apple growers, Broomfields, have a farm shop and tea room on the road up to Holt Heath.

18 RIVER SEVERN Bevere Lock 4mls/11k/1hr

THE Malvern Hills come into view in the neighbourhood of Bevere, glimpsed on the south-west horizon behind the spire of Hallow church. Queen Elizabeth I is said to have hunted for deer hereabouts. Another historical figure, albeit a peripheral one, with associations in the area was Napoleon's brother, Lucien Bonaparte, who lived in exile near Grimley for a period of time.

Make the most of your brief encounter with the Severn. For unless you choose to tie up, perhaps - if there is room - at Bevere or Holt locks, or at one of the riparian hostelries, like the incomparable Camp House - the three or four hours spent on the river between Worcester and Stourport are apt to flash swiftly by, leaving you with just a treasured blur of alder and willow fringed banks broken by occasional outcrops of sandstone; caravan parks and static homes; cattle or anglers flank or thigh high in the river margin; kingfishers skimming like low flying aircraft over the water's surface; and the unruffled routine of the automated locks.

A loop in the river forms the three acre island of Bevere, a place of refuge for the good burghers of Worcester in medieval times when war or plague threatened. Just upstream, the revitalised Droitwich (Barge) Canal departs to the east, climbing through eight broadbeam locks to the former salt-making town which lends it its name, thence continuing as the narrowbeam Droitwich Junction Canal to meet the Worcester & Birmingham Canal at Hanbury Wharf - see Map 15. Coverage of this Mid-Worcestershire mini-ring can be found in the seventh edition of the *Severn & Avon Canal & River Companion*.

Opened in 1771 and surveyed by Brindley - though actually engineered by John Priddey - the Droitwich Barge Canal flourished during the 19th century as an export route for the salt industry, an activity carried out in the vicinity since Roman times. When salt making declined this 'barge' canal fell into decay and was disused by the time of the First World War, its horse-drawn trows just a memory. In 1973 a trust was formed to restore the canal, and three decades and £12 million later their laudable ambition has borne fruit.

The village of Grimley sits well back from the river, though anglers make use of the bumpy lane down to the water's edge to reach their perches in amongst the musky clumps of balsam. In the winter months cormorants occupy the high, skeletal branches of riverside trees, an image reminiscent of a Japanese print.

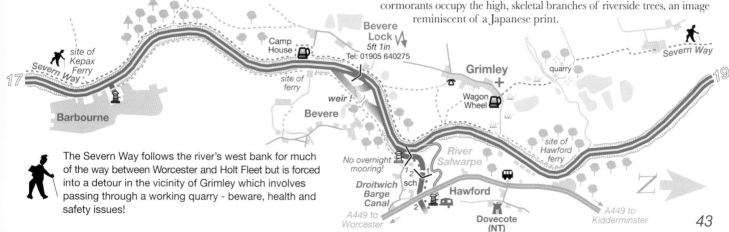

The Severn Way follows the river's west bank for much of the way between Worcester and Holt Fleet but is forced into a detour in the vicinity of Grimley which involves passing through a working quarry - beware, health and safety issues!

19 RIVER SEVERN Holt Fleet 4.5mls/11k/1hr

IN his 1949 topographical guide to the county of Worcestershire, L. T. C. Rolt suggested that "anyone so disposed could forget the present in Shrawley Woods," going on to evoke two halcyon summer days moored aboard *Cressy* along this most beautiful of upper navigable Severn reaches between Holt and Lincomb locks.

Disregard for the present implies a nostalgia for the past, and it is intriguing to discover that Dick Brook - emerging almost imperceptibly out of the shadowy trees on the west bank of the river - was once made navigable in the 17th century to serve a forge located deep in the woods. Two lock chambers were cut out of the sandstone, and cargoes of pig iron brought up from the

Forest of Dean were probably transhipped into tub boats to be conveyed along the narrow stream to the doors of the forge. The brain behind this was Andrew Yarranton, a Brindley before his time.

The Holts provide vestiges of civilisation alongside the river's otherwise remote course: Holt, Holt Heath, Holt Fleet and, just off the edge of our map, Holt Who Goes There? A rash of caravan parks and shanty-like chalets mar otherwise unspoilt riverside meadows for everyone but their proud owners. Luckily this manifestation of mankind's capacity for destroying the very tranquillity he desires is confined to those parts of the river nearest main roads. Holt Fleet is such a place, apt to bristle with 'Brummies' on sunny weekends, and yet Telford's dignified (and recently

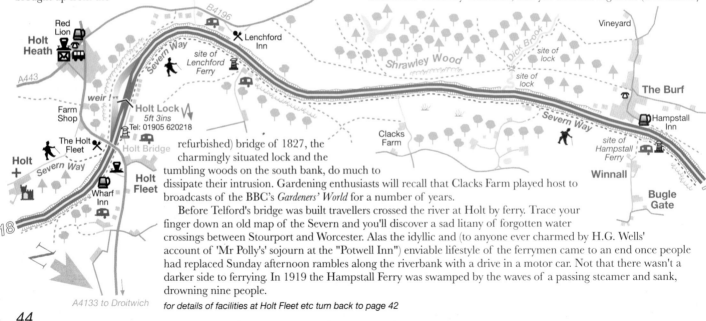

refurbished) bridge of 1827, the charmingly situated lock and the tumbling woods on the south bank, do much to dissipate their intrusion. Gardening enthusiasts will recall that Clacks Farm played host to broadcasts of the BBC's *Gardeners' World* for a number of years.

Before Telford's bridge was built travellers crossed the river at Holt by ferry. Trace your finger down an old map of the Severn and you'll discover a sad litany of forgotten water crossings between Stourport and Worcester. Alas the idyllic and (to anyone ever charmed by H.G. Wells' account of 'Mr Polly's' sojourn at the "Potwell Inn") enviable lifestyle of the ferrymen came to an end once people had replaced Sunday afternoon rambles along the riverbank with a drive in a motor car. Not that there wasn't a darker side to ferrying. In 1919 the Hampstall Ferry was swamped by the waves of a passing steamer and sank, drowning nine people.

for details of facilities at Holt Fleet etc turn back to page 42

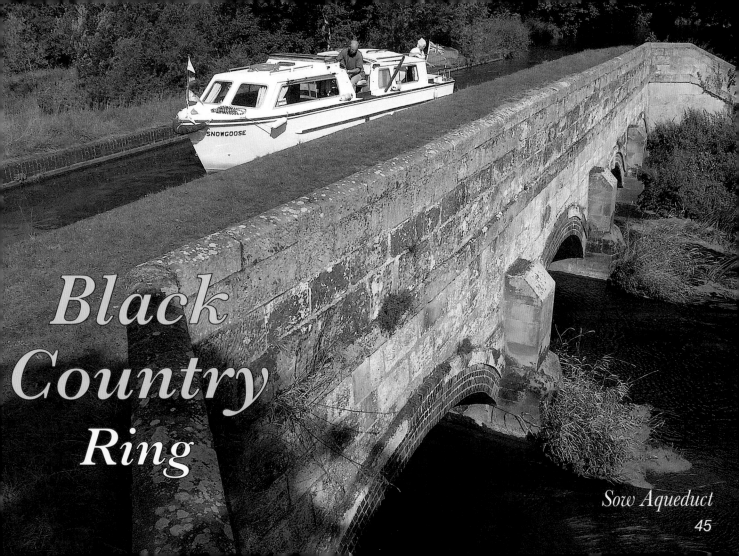

Black Country Ring

Sow Aqueduct

WITH twenty-four locks to contend with in less than three miles, the Birmingham & Fazeley Canal's departure from (or approach to) Birmingham makes considerable demands upon the boater's reservoir of energy. Farmer's Bridge Locks are an object lesson in urban regeneration. Not that long ago they were a largely inaccessible eyesore - a boil, if you like, on Birmingham's bottom - suffering from years of neglect following the demise of commercial carrying in the early nineteen-sixties. In 1984 a programme of renewal commenced. Using Gas Street Basin to Aston Junction as a prototype, the towpath was resurfaced, access improved, landscaping and lighting undertaken to the tune of a then not inconsiderable total of a million pounds. The scheme's impact was palpable. It introduced Brummies to a well-kept secret aspect of their city and they soon discovered it in droves. Nowadays

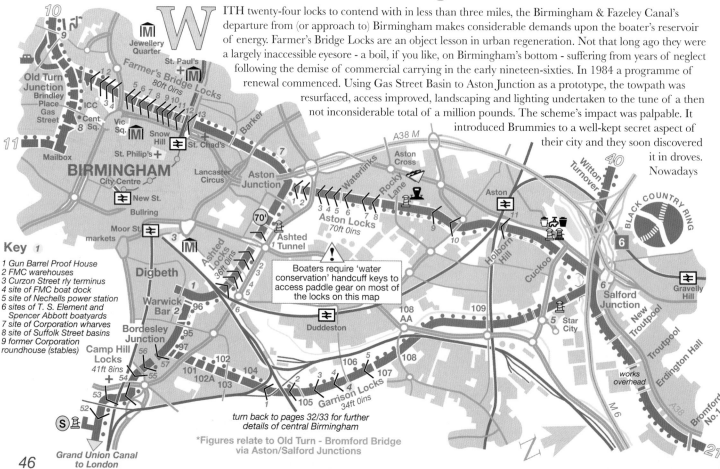

Key 1

1 Gun Barrel Proof House
2 FMC warehouses
3 Curzon Street rly terminus
4 site of FMC boat dock
5 site of Nechells power station
6 sites of T. S. Element and
Spencer Abbott boatyards
7 site of Corporation wharves
8 site of Suffolk Street basins
9 former Corporation
roundhouse (stables)

Boaters require 'water conservation' handcuff keys to access paddle gear on most of the locks on this map

turn back to pages 32/33 for further details of central Birmingham

*Figures relate to Old Turn - Bromford Bridge via Aston/Salford Junctions

it hooches with shop and office staff on warm weekday lunchtimes and family groups on postprandial Sunday walks. Joggers relish it too, extending their limbs and expending their energy up and down the ribbed brick surfaces of the refurbished towpath in a distant echo of the hurrying boatmen of the past.

Farmer's Bridge Locks

Farmer's Bridge Locks pass dramatically beneath the commercial core of the city. Each time we visit here more change has accrued: redeveloping the redeveloped one might put it. Alongside Lock 6 lie the offices of Mitchell & Butler, their iconic Birmingham brewing heritage exchanged for a portfolio of restaurant and bar chains. Locks 10 and 11 lie in a cavern beneath British Telecom's communications tower. There's access to Ludgate Hill and the calm oasis of St Paul's Square, nicknamed the 'Jeweller's Church' because of its connections with the adjoining Jewellery Quarter, a fascinating corner of old Birmingham. Between Locks 12 and 13 the canal negotiates a stygian vault under Snow Hill railway station; closed and subsequently demolished at some cost in 1972, but re-opened and rebuilt at more cost (though markedly less flamboyance) just fifteen years later.

Lock 13 marks the foot of the flight. Nearby - all but obscured from the canal - stands St Chad's, Pugin's Roman Catholic Cathedral of 1841. Between Snow Hill and Aston the canal, clear of locks for a brief respite, widens and is less claustrophobically engulfed by the high canyons of industry and commerce. The most significant feature of this section - apart from the switchback side bridges which formerly gave access to the Corporation wharves - is the handsome Barker Bridge, a graceful span of cast iron supported by brick piers and abutments dating from 1842.

Aston Locks

A Horseley Iron Works cast iron roving bridge marks the junction of the Birmingham & Fazeley Canal with the Digbeth Branch at Aston. Its

elegance, amounting almost to a misleading fragility, is in marked contrast to the overpowering concrete edifice of the adjacent Expressway. Time and time again exploration of the BCN emphasises the great gulf in aesthetic achievement between the civil engineering of the nineteenth century and the twentieth. Time alters perception, but it does seem inconceivable that any age will ever be able to indentify beauty in the Aston Expressway.

By Rocky Lane Bridge are offside visitor moorings and access to a small convenience store and take-away. Up the road at Aston Cross the HP sauce factory site has been adapted as a vast Asian cash & carry. Access to and from the canal is provided at Holborn Hill Bridge. Easy, then, to use Aston railway station as a staging post: a five minute train ride out from New Street followed by a healthy hour's walk back along the towpath to the city centre. Nearby, one of the earliest main line railways crosses the canal by Lock 11. Opened in 1837, only fifty years after the canal, it linked Birmingham with the North-west. Moorings and boating facilities are provided by Cuckoo Bridge.

Salford Junction

Only a fraction of the stressed-out motorists, fighting their way around the confusion of Gravelly Hill Interchange (aka Spaghetti Junction) are aware of the older, less frenzied meeting and parting of ways engulfed in the concrete gloom below. But such is Salford Junction, where the Grand Union Canal's 'Saltley Cut' and Tame Valley Canal - both dating from 1844 - form a canal crossroads with the Birmingham & Fazeley Canal. It's a sobering spot for contemplating Man's contribution to the landscape. Monstrously compromised, the River Tame churns despondently through artificial channels beneath successive generations of roads. But nature is undaunted: coots and yellow wagtails search assiduously for their next meal in the shallow margins of the river. Where the Cross-City railway crosses the Tame Valley Canal near Witton Turnover Bridge, a memorial

continued overleaf:

47

continued from page 47:

marks the spot where a policeman died after being stabbed in 2004. Whilst Aston Locks represent the most obvious, time efficient route for boaters tackling the "Black Country Ring", a fascinating alternative for die-hards (or indeed as part of a self-contained circular itinerary on foot or afloat) can be made up out of the Digbeth Branch and Grand Union Canal via Bordesley and Saltley as described below.

The Digbeth Branch

Opened in 1799, the Digbeth Branch descends through half a dozen locks from Aston Junction to Warwick Bar, terminating in a pair of foreshortened basins once lucratively busy with trade to and from Digbeth's many food factories like Typhoo Tea and HP Sauce. It used to be a secretive section of urban canal of unique character and appeal, but revelopment of Birmingham's 'Eastside' is relentlessly exorcizing the past. All but the top lock have extended side pounds, whilst the chambers have single gates top and bottom as per BCN practice. 48 hour visitor moorings are to be found in the relative security and calm of Aston Science Park with a handy winding hole nearby.

The advent of HS2, pencilled in for 2026, is viewed as a catalyst for regeneration hereabouts. Meanwhile, the original sandstone arch of the Grand Junction Railway's line provides a portal into a curvaceous, sepulchral 'tunnel' of railway lines, beyond which the canal opens out to Digbeth (or Proof House) Junction. The alternative name - also used by the adjoining maze of railway tracks - reflects the proximity of the Gun Barrel Proof House of 1813, a strikingly handsome building, with a Jacobean air, overlooking a cobbled courtyard. Above the entrance door is a colourful, three-dimensional military sculpture and the inscription: "Established by Act of Parliament for Public Security."

Warwick Bar & Bordesley Junction

Whereas the 'Worcester Bar' at Gas Street lies on a well-trodden tourist trail, the 'Warwick Bar' in Digbeth lies off the beaten track in a 'backstreet' Birmingham which plays host to a gallimaufry of workshops and lock-ups. A stop lock was constructed to separate the valuable waters of the Birmingham & Fazeley (later BCN) and Warwick & Birmingham canal companies. But whilst the environs and towpath received cosmetic attention in the recent past, vandalism has already negated the effort put in. As with Iraq and Afganistan, if you're determined to make an improvement, you have to maintain a presence to police it.

Alongside the remains of the stop lock stands a warehouse with an awning supported by cast-iron pillars over an arm lying parallel to the narrows. At one time it was leased by Geest the fruit importers and earned the sobriquet 'Banana Warehouse'. Earlier still it belonged to Pickfords, canal carriers of some importance before they made their name with heavy road transport. Nearby is New Warwick Wharf, marked by the tall curved wall of Fellows, Morton & Clayton's warehouse built in 1935 following modernisation of the canal from London. This confident 'Art Deco' style of architecture - emblazoned with the company's name along Fazeley Street to this day - was not rewarded by a significant increase in trade, and, having been for a number of years used by HP Sauce, it now houses a conglomeration of small businesses. Likewise FMC's adjoining Fazeley Street depot, separated from the newer building by an aqueduct over the turgid waters of the River Rea. Built of alternate courses of red and blue brick, and equipped with weatherboarded elevators and an attractive saw-tooth valanced canopy over a side arm, this older grouping of warehouses has been redeveloped as 'The Bond', a centre for graphic art based businesses. Directly opposite the towpath rises and falls over a side bridge spanning an arm which once led into one of the City of Birmingham's Salvage Department basins. Horsedrawn rubbish boats operated between here and the Small Heath destructor until 1965. The high arch of a ruined railway viaduct (which never carried trains) frames the canal near Bridge 95.

The Saltley Cut

Surrounded by gloomy factory walls, Bordesley Junction is spanned by a graceful roving bridge cast by Lloyds & Fosters. Immediately southwards the Grand Union Canal commences the climb to its Olton Summit via Camp Hill Locks, a route covered in our *South Midlands Canal Companion*. Likewise the Saltley Cut, barely industrial now as neat blocks of new housing overlook a towpath burgeoning with poppies, cranesbill, dog rose and daisies: a fecundity derived from generations of boat horse dung perhaps.

MINWORTH used to mark the frontier between open country and the West Midlands conurbation, but the building of a high tech business park on the towpath side between Minworth Green and Wigginshill Road bridges has blurred the once distinct boundary. Corn fields remain defiantly agricultural on the opposite bank, but the more cynical may feel that it is only a matter of time before the prices for building land outweigh the marginal profits of the annual harvest.

If, then, you want to avoid overnight mooring in a built-up area, you would be advised to tie up no further west than Wigginshill Road Bridge. A pleasant stroll can be had from here up past the Jacobean gabled farmhouse of Wiggins Hill Farm and beyond to where you come upon a picturesque (if converted) barn built of brick and timber.

Not that the stretch of canal between Bromford and Minworth is uninteresting. Reference to three twentieth century maps revealed a steady cycle of change. In 1916 the tyre makers Dunlop built a huge works on a 400 acre greenfield site which became known as Fort Dunlop. To transport the workforce to and from this new plant, the company operated a small fleet of passenger carrying narrowboats between Aston and Bromford until the neighbouring Tyburn Road was laid with tram tracks. Apparently the two and a half mile, lock-free journey took around half an hour and each boat could seat a hundred passengers. The imposing 'Art Deco' Cincinnati Machine Company's premises by

Minworth Top lock formerly manufactured lathes and profiling equipment. Now it has been acquired by Urban Splash for redevelopment.

In 1938 the fields east of Fort Dunlop were occupied by one of the 'shadow' munitions factories as Britain armed for war. During the next seven years over eleven thousand Spitfires were built at the plant. The works was handily placed for test flights, for across the Chester Road stood Castle Bromwich Aerodrome which had hosted Birmingham's very first flying demonstration in 1911. After the Second World War the aerodrome was run down and replaced, in the early Sixties, by the sprawling estate of Castle Vale.

In his books *Number One* and *Following the Trade*, former canal boat captain, Tom Foxon, recalls his experiences on the Birmingham & Fazeley in the mid 1950s. At that time substantial tonnages of coal were still being carried by canal from the collieries of North Warwickshire to the factory furnaces of Birmingham aboard 'Joey boats', boatman's parlance for narrowboats used for short-haul work and not designed for living aboard. The men who worked these largely horse-drawn boats knew this canal as the 'Old Cut' and in his book Tom describes the working practices of the era, commenting wryly that this was the most depressing route experienced in his boating career. You'll just have to take it from us that matters have improved since those days - well relatively! Near Minworth Green narrowboats used to unload ash for use in the filter beds of the adjoining sewage plant.

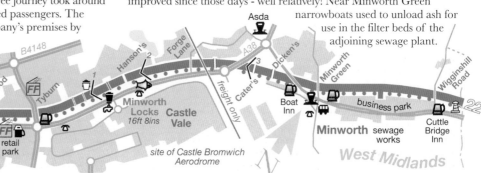

22 BIRMINGHAM & FAZELEY CANAL Curdworth 4mls/11lks/3hrs

WHO loves the Birmingham & Fazeley? It's not the most charismatic of canals, though it certainly provides a useful link between the canals of the east and west midlands, and is a constituent of the popular Black Country and Warwickshire 'rings'. Here, spending five miles or so in the company of the county of Warwickshire, it traverses a largely agricultural landscape pockmarked with abandoned gravel pits. The M42 motorway runs parallel to the canal and the M6 Toll road crosses it, its construction necessitating repositioning of the Top Lock and replacement of the lock-keeper's house at Dunton Wharf. The canal cottages along this length are numbered in the BCN sequence, a reminder that the B&F merged with the Birmingham Canal Navigations in 1794. The lock flight itself is maintained in an exemplary fashion, and flower beds enhance many of the chambers, though the towpath could do with improving.

Gravel has been extracted from the valley of the Tame since the 1930s. Originally by dredger, later by dragline. Nowadays conveyor belts carry the minerals to screening and washing plants where they are sorted into varying types of aggregates. The landscape might have been irrevocably scarred by such activities were it not for the imaginative creation of Kingsbury Water Park out of the abandoned gravel workings. Moorings are available above the bottom lock and it's but a short walk to the park's Visitor Centre.

Middleton Hall was the home of two eminent naturalists, Francis Willoughby and John Ray. Queen Elizabeth stayed here in 1567, her retinue lustily eating their way through sixty-nine beef cattle, one hundred and twenty-eight sheep, and two thousand chickens during the course of a week. In recent years the property has been painstakingly restored by the Middleton Hall Trust and is open to the public on Sundays and Bank holidays between Easter and September.

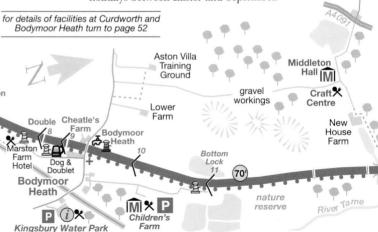

for details of facilities at Curdworth and Bodymoor Heath turn to page 52

Not far north from Dunton Wharf, along the A446 is the Belfry Hotel and its famous golf course, scene of many a nail-biting Ryder Cup denouement. Another sporting association belongs to Bodymoor Heath where Aston Villa, the illustrious Birmingham football club, have their impressive training ground.

The bottom lock of the Curdworth flight is overlooked by a quartet of canal cottages. Life must be pleasant here if, as one supposes, the inhabitants find the isolation conducive. Skeins of geese rise into the wide skies from flooded gravel workings.

50

FAZELEY JUNCTION isn't anywhere near as pretty as Fradley, but it exudes a certain grubby grandeur, lent added gravitas by a big old textile mill which quite plausibly might have escaped from Oldham or Rochdale. The Birmingham & Fazeley reached here in 1789 and the following year Sir Robert Peel (father of the Prime Minister) opened a mill for cotton spinning and calico printing. A second mill, known as Tolson's, was erected in 1883. Within its five towering storeys its workforce engaged in the production of haberdashery and upholstery. And when they weren't beavering away at work, they ran their own concert band, delightfully known as Tolson's Music Weavers. It was heartening to discover that the handsome junction house, boarded up on the occasion of our last visit, has been offered a new lease of life.

South of Fazeley Junction the canal negotiates an area devoted to gravel extraction. From Fisher's Mill Bridge a bucolic footpath leads via a farm with pigs to Middleton Hall and its Craft Centre. Close to the entrance to Drayton Manor Park (including Thomas (the tank engine) Land) stands Drayton Footbridge, a gothic folly which can lay claim to being one of the 'little wonders' of the inland waterways. Have your camera ready! East of Fisher's Mill Bridge the RSPB are developing a nature reserve amidst former gravel workings.

From Fazeley, the Coventry Canal heads towards Glascote Locks and the outskirts of Tamworth, a route covered in Pearson's *South Midlands Canal Companion*. Northwards, the Coventry/Birmingham & Fazeley runs past the Canal & River Trust's regional offices at Peel's Wharf. There are glimpses to the north of Tamworth Castle and the imposing parish church of St Editha, before the canal escapes the clutches of the retail parks and loses itself in and amongst the cabbage fields - which it is often called upon to irrigate - on the way to Hopwas.

To the west looms a tall transmitting mast at Hints, erected as long ago as 1956 to broadcast the then fledgeling ITV Channel to the west midlands. Nearby, a new section of the A5 carves its way through the adjoining escarpment with scant consideration for the equilibrium of this otherwise rural locality. Follow the by-road west from Ball's Bridge, and you'll arrive (having crossed the B5404) on a hillside known enigmatically as 'The Devil's Dressing Room'. The story goes that stone from the hill was quarried during the construction of Lichfield Cathedral, and that devil-faced gargoyles were 'dressed' on site by stonemasons, hence the name. If nothing else, you'll enjoy an invigorating walk, and be rewarded by a fine view of the cathedral itself.

The Birmingham & Fazeley towpath is properly surfaced and in excellent condition between Birmingham and Minworth. Thereafter, however, it deteriorates apart from good sections in the vicinity of Fazeley and Hopwas. Walkers will not experience undue discomfort, but cyclists would be well advised to seek advice from CART's offices at Peel's Wharf open Mon-Fri 10am-2pm.

for details of facilities at Fazeley turn to page 52

Curdworth
Map 22

Curdworth is one of the oldest settlements in this part of the world and derives its name from Crida, the first King of Mercia. The Battle of Curdworth Bridge - reputedly the first skirmish of the Civil War - occurred here in August 1642.

Eating & Drinking
WHITE HORSE - adjacent Curdworth Bridge. Tel: 01675 470227. 'Vintage Inn'. B76 9DS

Shopping
Post Office stores in village on far side of A4079.

Bodymoor Heath
Map 22

Eating & Drinking
DOG & DOUBLET - canalside adjacent Cheatle's Farm Bridge. Tel: 01827 872374. Rambling Georgian pub with attractive interiors and garden with dovecot. B76 9JD

Things to Do
KINGSBURY WATER PARK - Over six hundred acres of waterside and woodland walks. Miniature railway rides on the extensive Echills Wood Railway. Cycle hire, cafe and gift shop, Tel: 01827 872660. Moorings above Bottom Lock. B76 0DY
BROOMEY CROFT CHILDREN'S FARM - Tel: 01827 873844. Not so much a genetically-modified approach to child-rearing, more a fun day for the family. Tractor & trailer rides. Tea rooms and gift shop. B76 0EE
MIDDLETON HALL & CRAFT CENTRE - Former home of Sir Hugh Willoughby the Tudor explorer. Tel: 01827 283095. Craft Centre Wed-Sun. Coffee Shop daily 11am-5pm. Tel: 01827 261414. B78 2AE

Fazeley
Map 23

Those mills set the door tone, aided and abetted by a mordant supporting cast: the United Methodist Free Church of 1884; the terracotta Parish Hall of 1897; workers' terraces, and a timber yard.

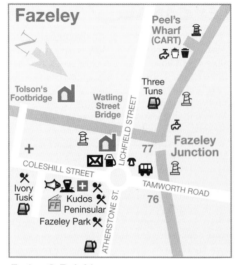

Eating & Drinking
THREE TUNS - Lichfield Street. Tel: 01827 259938. Homely Watling Street pub backing onto the canal with limited offside moorings for customers. B78 3QN
KUDOS - Coleshill Street. Tel: 01827 254777. Indian fusion restaurant. B78 3RB
IVORY TUSK - Coleshill Street. Tel: 01827 285777. *Another* Indian restaurant B78 3RG
FAZELEY PARK - Atherstone Street. Tel: 01827 261718. A *third* Indian! B78 3RF
PENINSULAR - Coleshill Street. Tel: 01827 288321. Chinese restaurant with take-away outlet. B78 3RB
Plus two other pubs, two more Chinese take-aways, and a fish & chip shop.

Shopping
There's a Tesco Express (with cash machine), pharmacy and post office in the petrol station. From Bonehill Bridge a footpath leads under the A5 to a nearby retail park featuring Asda and Sainsbury's supermarkets, Marks & Spencer, KFC and McDonald's et al.

Things to Do
DRAYTON MANOR THEME PARK - open daily Easter to October. Admission charge. Access on A4091 adjacent to Drayton footbridge. Tel: 0844 472 1950. 'Thomas Land', amusements, zoo, farm park, nature trail and woodland walk. B78 3SA

Connections
BUSES - frequent connections with Tamworth and its railhead. Tel: 0871 200 2233.

Hopwas
Map 24

18th Century river bridge, and 19th Century church (in Arts & Crafts style) and old waterworks.
TAME OTTER - canalside Lichfield Road Bridge. Tel: 01827 53361. 'Vintage Inn' with an entertaining pun to its name. B78 3AF
RED LION - canalside at Lichfield Road Bridge. Tel: 01827 62514. B78 3AF

Whittington
Map 24

Attractive village retaining a couple of pubs: BELL INN (Tel: 01543 432377 - WS14 9JR) and DOG INN (Tel: 01543 432601 - WS14 9JU). There is additionally a Chinese take-away - Tel: 01543 433397. Shopping facilities include a Co-op store, pharmacy, and post-office. Bus service 765 runs hourly (bi-hourly Suns) to both Lichfield and Tamworth.

Huddlesford
Map 24

THE PLOUGH - canalside Bridge 83. Tel: 01543 432369. Country pub with little garden where you can both boat-watch and train-watch simultaneously. Bar and restaurant food. WS13 8PY Good visitor moorings make Huddlesford a handy point for excursions into Lichfield. Lichfield Taxis - Tel: 01543 547979.

NOT generally thought of as a beautiful canal, the Coventry nevertheless becomes almost picturesque in its wandering between Fazeley and Huddlesford; particularly as it ghosts through the brackeny woodlands of Hopwas, where red flags warn of military manoeuvres. Glibly we call this the Coventry Canal, but actually - and by now the presence of nameplates and not numbers on the bridges should have quickened your suspicions - the canal between Fazeley and Whittington was built by the Birmingham & Fazeley company. The Coventry Canal received its Act of Parliament in 1768, but seventeen years later it was nowhere near completion; primarily through a shortage of capital, but also, historians suspect, because some of the directors had interests in the Warwickshire coalfield and were worried by the thought that their through route, were it to be finished, would boost trade from the North Staffordshire pits at the expense of their own. In frustration the Trent & Mersey and Birmingham & Fazeley companies undertook to jointly build the canal between Fazeley and Fradley. The two met at Whittington in 1790, at a point graced with a plaque provided by the local branch of the I.W.A. commemorating the bicentenary of the joining.

So pleasant scenery, Packington pigs and polytunnels mingle as you negotiate the lower valley of the Tame; passing Fisherwick, where the houses face the canal in Dutch fashion, rather than turning their backs on it as is more often the case in England. An ornate and enigmatic pair of gateposts stand alongside the telephone kiosk adjacent to Hademoor House Bridge. They formed one of the entrances to Fisherwick Hall, a mansion once couched in a Capability Brown landscape, but demolished as long ago as 1818 to pay off the gambling debts of its owner, the Marquess of Donegal. When the West Coast Main Line was recently quadrupled the level crossing at Hademoor was replaced by an overbridge. Equestrians are obliged to dismount in case the trains rushing beneath at a hundred and twenty-five miles an hour scare their steeds, so mounting-blocks are thoughtfully provided.

A signpost at Huddlesford points prophetically towards Ogley, anticipating restoration of the Wyrley & Essington Canal, abandoned half a century before the canal system's leisure renaissance gathered momentum. Championed by the Lichfield & Hatherton Canals Trust, the project envisages reinstatement of seven miles of canal including four detours from the original route in response to post-abandonment developments. Work has already commenced at a number of sites but the provision of expensive culverts beneath the A38 and A5 trunk roads remains a major challenge; though the erection of an aqueduct over the M6 toll road in 2003 illustrates the strength of commitment locally to such a potentially exciting scheme. Meanwhile, Lichfield Cruising Club use the first half mile of the W&E as linear moorings.

Map labels:
course of Wyrley & Essington Canal to Ogley Jnct.
by-road to Lichfield - 1 mile
84
25
Cappers Watery Lane
LCC B
83
Huddlesford Junction
Huddlesford
82
The Plough
81
80
79
78
cricket ground
Whittington
Whittington
IWA plaque
West Coast Main Line
A51 to Lichfield
former waterworks
St Chad's
Hopwas Hays Wood
Hademoor House
Hademoor Farm
Fisherwick
Hopwas
Lichfield Road
Dixon's
School
Wood
Tamhorn Park
Tamhorn House
Tamhorn Farm
70'
23
A51 to Tamworth
River Tame
N

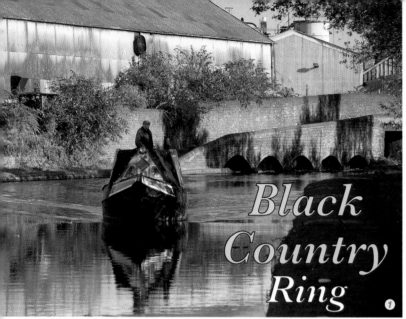

Black Country Ring

1 Smethwick
2 Tipton Traditional
3 Bilston Ducks
4 Deepfields Junction
5 Wolverhampton Shopper
6 Tixall Wide

54

1 Colwich Lock
2 'Old Thirteen'
3 Haywood Lock
4 Winson Green
5 Fradley Junction

OLD HILL BRIDGE N° 107

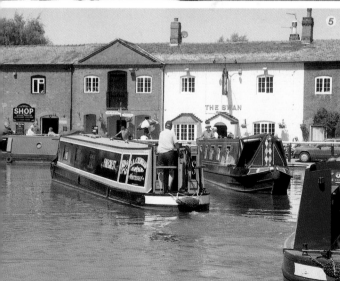

55

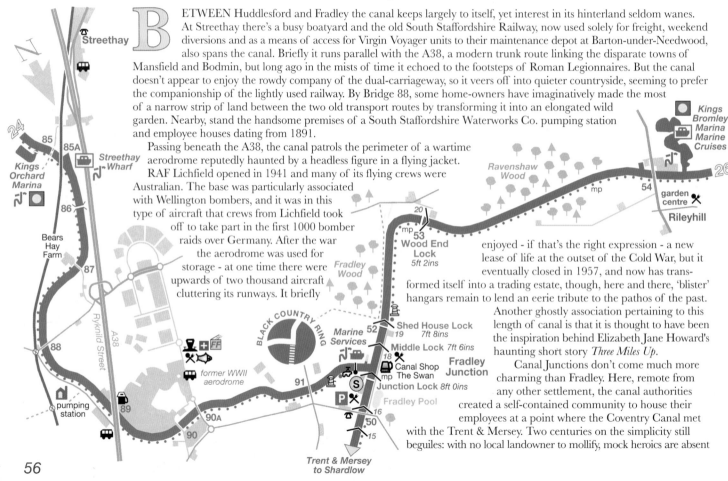

BETWEEN Huddlesford and Fradley the canal keeps largely to itself, yet interest in its hinterland seldom wanes. At Streethay there's a busy boatyard and the old South Staffordshire Railway, now used solely for freight, weekend diversions and as a means of access for Virgin Voyager units to their maintenance depot at Barton-under-Needwood, also spans the canal. Briefly it runs parallel with the A38, a modern trunk route linking the disparate towns of Mansfield and Bodmin, but long ago in the mists of time it echoed to the footsteps of Roman Legionnaires. But the canal doesn't appear to enjoy the rowdy company of the dual-carriageway, so it veers off into quieter countryside, seeming to prefer the companionship of the lightly used railway. By Bridge 88, some home-owners have imaginatively made the most of a narrow strip of land between the two old transport routes by transforming it into an elongated wild garden. Nearby, stand the handsome premises of a South Staffordshire Waterworks Co. pumping station and employee houses dating from 1891.

Passing beneath the A38, the canal patrols the perimeter of a wartime aerodrome reputedly haunted by a headless figure in a flying jacket. RAF Lichfield opened in 1941 and many of its flying crews were Australian. The base was particularly associated with Wellington bombers, and it was in this type of aircraft that crews from Lichfield took off to take part in the first 1000 bomber raids over Germany. After the war the aerodrome was used for storage - at one time there were upwards of two thousand aircraft cluttering its runways. It briefly enjoyed - if that's the right expression - a new lease of life at the outset of the Cold War, but it eventually closed in 1957, and now has transformed itself into a trading estate, though, here and there, 'blister' hangars remain to lend an eerie tribute to the pathos of the past.

Another ghostly association pertaining to this length of canal is that it is thought to have been the inspiration behind Elizabeth Jane Howard's haunting short story *Three Miles Up*.

Canal Junctions don't come much more charming than Fradley. Here, remote from any other settlement, the canal authorities created a self-contained community to house their employees at a point where the Coventry Canal met with the Trent & Mersey. Two centuries on the simplicity still beguiles: with no local landowner to mollify, mock heroics are absent

Map labels

Streethay
Kings Orchard Marina
85
85A
Streethay Wharf
86
Bears Hay Farm
87
Rykwild Street
A38
88
pumping station
89
90
90A
91
24
Kings Bromley Marina Marine Cruises
Ravenshaw Wood
mp
54
garden centre
Rileyhill
26
20
mp 53
Wood End Lock 5ft 2ins
Fradley Wood
BLACK COUNTRY RING
Marine Services
52 Shed House Lock 19 7ft 8ins
Middle Lock 7ft 6ins 18
Canal Shop mp The Swan
Junction Lock 8ft 0ins
Fradley Junction
Fradley Pool
S
P
16
50
15
former WWII aerodrome
Trent & Mersey to Shardlow

from the architecture. Solely in the Georgian junction house - home to the Company's 'man' - does style depart from the functional; though even then the effect is soberly restrained.

West of Fradley Junction, the Trent & Mersey Canal passes through woods richly coloured by rhododendrons in May and June. Wood End is the southernmost point of the canal in its 92 mile journey from Shardlow, by the Trent, to Preston Brook, near the Mersey. HS2 is earmarked to cross the canal hereabouts. There are glimpses, southwards, to the three spires of Lichfield Cathedral. By Kings Bromley Wharf stand the buildings of an old creamery (encountered in *Narrow Boat*) which once relied upon water transport in much the same way as that at Knighton on the Shropshire Union Canal. East of Fradley Junction the Trent & Mersey descends towards its brief mingling with the Trent at Alrewas - a route covered in our *South Midlands* and *Four Counties Ring* Canal Companions.

Fradley Junction — Map 25
Hugely popular midland canal centre.
Eating & Drinking
THE SWAN - canalside, Fradley Junction. Tel: 01283 790330. This former boatmen's pub plays a leading role in the social life of the Junction. DE13 7DN
CANALSIDE CAFE - cafe located in part of the former maintenance yard buildings. Outdoor canalside tables too. Tel: 01283 792508. DE13 7DN
KINGFISHER CAFE - cafe connected to holiday park. Tel: 01283 790407. DE13 7DN
Shopping
Groceries and gifts from the Canal Shop.
Connections
TAXIS - Alrewas Direct Cars. Tel: 01283 790373.

Handsacre — Map 26
The iron High Bridge, spanning the Trent to the north of Bridge 58, is well worth a sortie ashore.
Eating & Drinking
THE CROWN - Bridge 58. Tel: 01543 490003. Canalside pub; food from noon Tue-Sat. WS15 4DT
THE OLD PECULIER - village centre. Cosy local. Tel: 01543 491891. WS15 4DP
MICHAEL'S - The Green. Tel: 01543 491314. Lengthy queues for great ('Italian') fish & chips. WS15 4DT
Shopping
Convenience store and newsagent.

Armitage — Map 26
Offside moorings provide access via an alleyway to a goodly number of shops on the main road.
Eating & Drinking
PLUM PUDDING - canalside Bridge 61A. Tel: 01543 490330. Former canalside pub now an Italian restaurant open from noon daily. WS15 4AZ
ASH TREE - canalside Bridge 62. Tel: 01889 578314. Marston's 'Two for One' pub/restaurant. WS15 1PF
Shopping
Butcher, baker, post office, pharmacy, convenience store.
Connections
BUSES - Arriva service 825 as per Rugeley.

Rugeley — Map 27
Stoic little town which doesn't deserve to be cold-shouldered by canallers. The high-spired Catholic church is by Hansom, eponymous inventor of the horse-drawn cab. New miners statues on Globe traffic island.
Eating & Drinking
PLAZZA - Horsefair. Tel: 01889 586831. Wetherspoons characterfully housed in former cinema. WS15 2EJ
TERRAZZA - Lichfield Street. Tel: 01889 570630. Italian restaurant open Tue-Sat from 6.30pm. WS15 2EH
Shopping
Moor north of Bridge 66 for easiest access to town centre, Morrisons, Tesco and Aldi supermarkets. Market Hall and outdoor markets on Tue, Thur & Sat.

Connections
BUSES - Arriva service 825 (half-hourly Mon-Sat, hourly Sun) links Rugeley with Stafford (via Wolseley) and Lichfield (via Armitage and Handsacre) and is thus ideal for one-way towpath walks. Tel: 0871 200 2233.
TRAINS - useful hourly London Midland service along the Trent Valley and hourly from Town or Trent Valley stations to Walsall and Birmingham. Tel: 03457 484950.
TAXIS - Town & Country. Tel: 01889 576621.

Wolseley Bridge — Map 27
Wolseley has a craft centre, antiques showroom, wine merchant and garden centre (with cafe/restaurant) all accessible from Bridge 70.
Eating & Drinking
WOLSELEY ARMS - far side of river bridge. Tel: 01889 883179. Vintage Inns establishment, once the meeting place for the canal's promoters. ST17 0XS
SHIMLA PALACE - far side of river bridge by roundabout. Tel: 01889 881325. Indian restaurant, eat in or takeaway. Open from 5.30pm daily. ST17 0XS
Things to Do
THE WOLSELEY CENTRE - far side of river bridge beyond roundabout. Tel: 01889 880100. Staffordshire Wildlife Trust headquarters set in revitalised garden park: paths, hides and sensory garden. ST17 0WT
Connections
BUSES - Arriva service 825 as per Rugeley.

26 TRENT & MERSEY CANAL Handsacre & Armitage 4mls/0lks/1.5hrs

NORTH-WESTWARDS from Fradley the canal winds through a village-less tract of country, comprehensively agricultural now, but betraying signs of the wild heathland it must once have been in its sandy soil, gorse, bracken and gnarled oaks. From Bridge 58 it's but a short stroll to the old High Bridge across the Trent. Rendered obsolete by a contemporary concrete span entirely without aesthetic value, the older structure's contrastingly graceful cast iron span was made at Coalbrookdale in 1830. We're not convinced, however, that the bridge's current livery of dull maroon and green does it full justice. Nevertheless, it's pleasant to stand on the old bridge for awhile, watching the Trent flowing below, and wondering what's for tea.

Armitage and Shanks are synonymous with toilet plumbing, their trade marks are emblazoned on public conveniences throughout the world. Once they were separate firms - they merged in 1969 - but the site alongside the canal at Armitage dates back to 1817. Sanitaryware became a speciality in the 19th century under the management of Edward Johns - the origin of the Americanism 'going to the John'. Today the factory is part of the Ideal Standard group, a public limited company apparently flushed with unlimited success; though they may well wish to keep that in the closet. A path worth exploring leaves the towpath between bridges 60 and 61 and leads beneath the railway and over the Trent to the isolated settlement of Mavesyn Ridware. Not that there are any facilities when you get there, but sometimes you just feel an urge to turn your back on the canal.

Connections are apparent with another famous earthenware firm at Spode House and Hawkesyard Priory. Josiah Spode, a member of the North Staffordshire pottery family, left his house to a Dominican Order in 1893 and the monks proceeded to build a priory in the grounds. The buildings now house a conference centre whilst the grounds have been converted into a golf course.

Passing beneath the A513, the canal narrows and negotiates a rocky cutting. One-way working is the order of the day. This was formerly the site of Armitage (or "Plum Pudding") Tunnel, a dramatic, unlined bore through the rock face. Subsidence, brought about by coal mining, necessitated opening out of the tunnel, and concrete lining of the canal banks. Not that mining is any longer an activity associated with the area. Lea Hall Colliery (1960-1990) stood canalside by Bridge 63 and was, initially, a showcase pit for the NCB, much of its output making the shortest of journeys to an adjacent power station, closed itself in 2016. An industrial estate has replaced the colliery, Amazon being a notable occupant. One aspect of the mining life they couldn't entirely eradicate, however, was its workforce, and it is not unusual when boating the Trent & Mersey or walking its towpath in this vicinity to overhear the accents of Lanarkshire and Northumberland, counties from which many miners 'emigrated' to Rugeley.

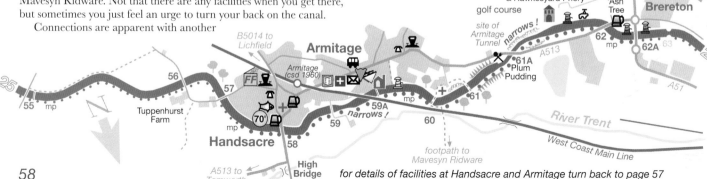

for details of facilities at Handsacre and Armitage turn back to page 57

27 TRENT & MERSEY CANAL Colwich & Rugeley 4mls/0lks/1.5hrs

THE river's slow influence pervades the canal, and the pair wander across the landscape like indolent lovers on a long afternoon, chaperoned at a discreet distance by the recumbent mass of The Chase. Several big houses were built by prosperous landowners in this enchanting countryside. The stuccoed facade of Bishton Hall overlooks the canal. Nowadays it is a prep school with a cricket ground shaded by ancient chestnut trees bordering the water. Intriguingly, it once boasted a Grecian boathouse on the banks of the Trent, the remains of which can be found amidst the undergrowth by a spill-weir. Another mansion, Wolseley Hall, stood opposite on the far bank of the river. It was demolished long ago, but the grounds have become home to a wildlife centre.

Wolseley Bridge has graced the Trent here since 1800. It was designed by John Rennie, best known in canal circles for his work on the Kennet & Avon. The Staffordshire Way joins the towpath at Bridge 68 and follows the canal as far as Great Haywood, before disappearing off into the grounds of Shugborough on its way to the southernmost tip of the county at Kinver Edge. On foot, Kinver is thus approximately forty miles and

about fifteen hours away; by boat the respective figures are a not dissimilar thirty-six miles and eighteen hours.

Rugeley gets a bad press from most guide-books which condescend to mention it at all, but we have always had a soft spot for this down to earth little town, formerly known for its tanneries; as the home of the notorious Victorian poisoner, William Palmer, and as the scene, in 1839, of the canal murder of Christina Collins. In the churchyard of St Augustine's (adjacent Bridge 67) an isolated gravestone marks her last resting place, noting that 'having been most barbarously treated was found dead in the Canal in this parish on 17th June 1839'. The story behind her misadventure - for which two boatmen were hung publicly at Stafford Gaol - inspired Colin Dexter's Inspector Morse story *The Wench is Dead*.

At Brindley Bank the canal suddenly stops running parallel to the Trent and turns sharply to cross it. Once there was a transhipment wharf here where flint was swapped between canal and river vessels for the short run down to Colton Mill by Trent Valley railway station. By Bridge 68 a short reedy arm adjacent to the railway provides a useful turning point for lengthy craft. It occurs to us that this may have been used as a transhipment basin in the fledgling days of the railway, perhaps for the conveyance of building materials.

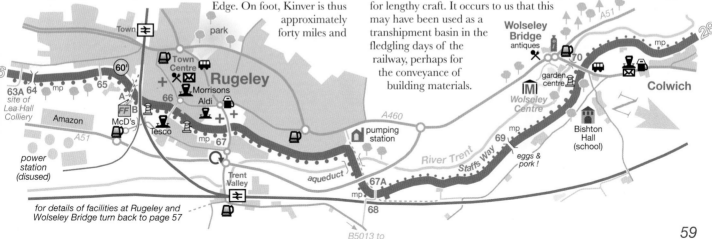

for details of facilities at Rugeley and Wolseley Bridge turn back to page 57

28 T&M and S&W CANALS Great Haywood 5mls/3lks/2.5hrs

BRINDLEY invariably found it simpler to follow river valleys, and Great Haywood was an obvious choice of location for a canal junction designed to establish his scheme for a 'Grand Cross' of man-made waterways linking the four great English estuaries: Humber, Thames, Severn and Mersey. With the completion of the Staffordshire & Worcestershire Canal in 1772, and the Trent & Mersey five years later, Haywood became a canal junction of major importance, as significant to transport in the 18th century as any motorway interchange today. One is only left to marvel at the simplicity of it all - two quiet ribbons of water meeting beneath a bridge of exquisite beauty - and compare it wistfully with transport interchanges of the 21st century, acres of concrete, noise and pollution. Where did we go wrong? History may have taken some wrong turnings, but there is little chance for the canal traveller to make a mistake, for a prominent fingerpost directs one concisely enough to "Wolverhampton", "The Trent", or "The Potteries". Between here and Colwich the Trent & Mersey is at its most memorably beautiful as it skirts the boundary of Shugborough. On one bank beechwoods tumble down to the water's edge. On the other, across the Trent, there are glimpses of the statues, antiquities and follies which pepper the grounds of this famous home of the Anson family.

Severn Springs

Cannock Chase

A513

Colwich Lock
6ft 6ins
21
71
71A
72
Colwich (csd 1958)
St Mary's Abbey
Little Haywood
River Trent
Staffs Way
mp
27

Triumphal Arch
farm & mill
Tower of the Winds

Staffs Way

River Sow

Milford & Brocton (csd 1950)
Milford
cricket ground
aqueduct
105 Milford
A513

Tixall Lock
4ft 3ins
106 Tixall
107 Oldhill
104 Walton
103 Stoneford
102

Tixall Wide

Tixall
Tixall Gatehouse

Great Haywood
72A
Essex Bridge
Gt Haywood (csd 1947)
22
73 Haywood Lock
4ft 2ins
Shugborough Hall & County Museum
109
Swivel 108
Haywood Junction
74
mp

BLACK COUNTRY RING

Trent & Mersey Canal to Stoke-on-Trent

Great Haywood

Essex Bridge
73
Haywood Lock
109
aqueducts
74
Anglo Welsh
farm shop
T&M
S&W
sewage works

N

29

60

Colwich Lock lies in an attractive setting between the village church, a picturesque farm, and a bend in the river. From Bridge 72 you can take an idyllic walk to Severn Springs, springboard for Cannock Chase. Hidden from the canal, but visible from passing trains, St Mary's Abbey is occupied by a small order of Benedictine nuns who can trace their origins back to 17th Century France and an English order based in Cambrai.

The Staffordshire & Worcestershire Canal

Through the arch of Bridge 109 - an 18th century fusion of functional engineering and enduring loveliness - the Staffordshire & Worcestershire Canal commences its 46 mile journey down to the Severn at Stourport. Two aqueducts carry it across the Trent and a millstream. A couple of miles further on it crosses the Sow. Between these river crossings the canal suddenly casts off its inhibitions and widens into a broad lake of quite un-canal-like proportions, bordered by thick reedbeds inhabited by a gorgeous array of wildfowl. Boaters will find their craft looping the loop out of sheer exuberance. This is Tixall Wide or Broadwater and there are two theories for its surprising existence. Some maintain that the canal was widened into an artificial lake to placate the owner of Tixall Hall. Others that the expanse of water predates the canal, that it was naturally formed, and that Izaak Walton learnt to fish here. Whichever explanation suits you, don't miss the extraordinary Elizabethan gatehouse which overlooks the Wide. The hall itself, where Mary Queen of Scots was imprisoned for a fortnight in 1586, was demolished long ago. The gatehouse (in the opinion of L. T. C. Rolt, a 'monstrosity'!) is let for holidays by the Landmark Trust.

West of Tixall's solitary lock the canal meanders enchantingly through the valley of the Sow. The river is crossed by way of a typical low-slung Brindley masonry aqueduct. Bridge 105 is a handsome turnover affair from which there is access under the railway to the village of Milford and access to Cannock Chase. Between here and Baswich the canal runs through fields between the river and the railway whose southbound trains are quickly gobbled up by the decorated portal of Shugborough Tunnel. Those of a railway bent may be intrigued to learn that Francis William Webb, the great locomotive engineer of the London & North Western Railway, hailed from Tixall, where his father was Rector for over half a century.

The Haywoods   Map 28

The villages of Great and Little Haywood are separated by a long, high make-work wall. Dormitory housing has inevitably expanded both populations, but the centres remain peaceful and largely unspoilt; especially so in the charming lane leading from Great Haywood, under the railway and over the canal, to the Essex Bridge, one of the finest examples of a packhorse bridge imaginable. Tolkien convalesced in Great Haywood after catching trench fever during the Battle of the Somme, and it is thinly disguised as Tavrobel in *The Tale of The Sun and The Moon*. It is further suggested that the rivers Gruir and Afros, which feature in that story, were inspired by the Trent and Sow.

Eating & Drinking

LOCK HOUSE - adjacent Haywood Lock. Tel: 01889 881294. Popular canalside tea rooms. ST18 0ST *Plus two pubs in Little Haywood and one in Great H.*

Shopping

Little Haywood has a convenience store. Great Haywood has two convenience stores (one with butcher's and post office counters), a pharmacy, and a farm shop (with butchery and cafe) alongside the junction. Laundry (and other boating) facilities are available at Great Haywood Marina which is located just off the edge of the map on the Trent & Mersey north of Haywood Junction.

Things to Do

SHUGBOROUGH - access via Haywood Lock and Essex Bridge. Open daily April to December. Admission charge. Attractions include mansion, county museum, working farm, watermill, gardens, National Trust shop and cafeteria. A visit to the farm can be particularly recommended for families. Special events and a regular point of departure for hot air balloons. Tel: 01889 881388 ST17 0XB

Connections

BUSES - Arriva service 825 operates half-hourly Mon-Sat (hourly Sun) from Little Haywood to Stafford and Lichfield via Rugeley. D&G services 841/2 connect Great Haywood with Stafford and Rugeley Mon-Sat. Tel: 0871 200 2233.

Milford   Map 28

Traditionally a motorist's gateway to Shugborough and The Chase, Milford now has the benefit of a mountain bike hire facility (Mammoth - Tel: 01785 664555 ST17 0UW) should canallers feel the need to swap modes for a bit. Other facilities include the Barley Mow (a Greene King Eating Inn - Tel: 01785 665230 ST17 0UW), The Viceroy (an Indian restaurant and take-away - Tel: 01785 663239 - ST17 0UH) and, bizarrely, Britain's most long-lived Wimpy fast food outlet. The easiest access to all theses facilities is along a track which leads beneath the railway from Bridge 105.

Stafford
Map 29

One of England's lesser-known county towns, Stafford has always seemed too self-effacing for its own good; though there are signs that in recent years it has begun to wake up to its tourist potential. Unfortunately for canal folk, the centre lies over a mile from Radford Bridge. But there are frequent buses, and those with time at their disposal will find Stafford a rewarding place to visit. First stop should be the Ancient High House in Greengate Street - the main thoroughfare. Dating from 1595, it's thought to be the largest timber-framed town house remaining in England. Inside there's a heritage exhibition tracing Stafford's history since 913 when Ethelfleda, daughter of Alfred the Great, fortified the settlement against marauding Danish invaders. King Charles I stayed at High House in 1642, and in later years Izaak Walton visited relatives who owned it. An alleyway beguiles you off Greengate Street to discover the town's large parish church of St Mary, much restored by Gilbert Scott in the 1840s and containing a bust of Izaak Walton. Another delightful church worth visiting is St Chad's on Greengate Street. Elsewhere, some impressive buildings reflect the town's administrative status.

Eating & Drinking
RADFORD BANK - canalside Bridge 98. Tel: 01785 242825. Crown Carvery. ST17 4PG
THE SOUP KITCHEN - Church Lane. Tel: 01785 254775. Open 9am-5pm Mon-Sat. Quaint, sprawling eatery (enhanced by attentive waitresses) serving coffees, lunches and teas. Rooftop garden. ST16 2AW

Shopping
Good shopping centre featuring all the well known 'high street' names plus many attractive individual shops tucked away down twisting side streets. Large Asda and Tesco supermarkets. Indoor market

(Earl Street) Tue, Thur, Fri & Sat. Farmers' Market on the second Saturday in the month. Convenience store accessible from Bridge 100 at Baswich. New Aldi supermarket near Bridge 98.

Things to Do
TOURIST INFORMATION - Gatehouse Theatre, Market Street. Tel: 01785 619619. ST16 2LT
ANCIENT HIGH HOUSE - Greengate Street. Tel: 01785 619131. Local history and gifts. ST16 2JA
SHIRE HALL GALLERY - Market Square. Tel: 01785 278345. Exhibitions, crafts and coffee bar housed in an imposing late Georgian building overlooking the Market Square. ST16 2LD
STAFFORD CASTLE - Tel: 01785 257698. Preserved Norman remains on western outskirts. ST16 1DJ

Connections
BUSES - services throughout the district. No.s 1,2,3,74 & 825 connect Radford (Bridge 98) at frequent intervals with the town centre. Tel: 0871 200 2233.
TAXIS - AJ's Tel: 01785 252255.
TRAINS - Important railhead with wide variety of services. Tel: 03457 484950. Useful links with Penkridge and Rugeley for clued-up towpath walkers.

Acton Trussell
Map 29

THE MOAT HOUSE - canalside Bridge 92. Tel: 01785 712217. Four star hotel in former moated farmhouse: restaurant and bars, lovely gardens. ST17 0RG

Penkridge
Map 30

A not uninteresting little town, and a good place to break your journey on the northern section of the Staffs & Worcs. Five minutes walk from the wharf will take you to the narrow main street, a pleasant spot to shop and saunter. At its foot - but mind the traffic on the A449 - stands St Michael's, an impressive church of sandstone, and formerly a collegiate church, considered second only to a cathedral in status.

Eating & Drinking
CROSS KEYS - canalside Bridge 84. Tel: 01785 712826. A once isolated pub, described by Rolt in *Narrow Boat*, but now surrounded by a housing estate. ST19 5HJ
THE BOAT - Bridge 86. Tel: 01785 715170. Canalside pub which has thankfully replaced its tanker barge sign with a more appropriate narrowboat. ST19 5DT
FLAMES - Mill Street. Tel: 01785 712955. Contemporary Eastern cuisine housed in one of Penkridge's most historic buildings. ST19 5AY

Shopping
Convenience shops by bridges 84 and 86. The town centre, with its Co-op supermarket and other retailers, is 5 minutes walk from the canal. Down by the river, the outdoor market operates on Wednesdays and Saturdays.

Connections
BUSES - Arriva service 76 runs hourly to Wolverhampton and Stafford. Tel: 0871 200 2233.
TRAINS - hourly London Midland services to Wolverhampton and Stafford. Tel: 03457 484950.
TAXIS - Aves. Tel: 01785 335044.

Coven
Map 32

Coven's village centre is less than ten minutes walk from Bridge 71, but do take care crossing the A449!

Eating & Drinking
FOX & ANCHOR - canalside north of Bridge 71. Tel: 01902 798786. Flourishing Vintage Inns establishment offering a wide choice of food and drink. WV9 5BX
Fish & chip shop, pub and cafe in the village centre.

Shopping
Co-op foodstore, butcher (on the road in) bakery, pharmacy, and post office. Secondhand bookshop adjoining the butcher, open Thur-Sat 11.30am - 4pm. Tel: 01902 791833.

LARGELY unmolested, the canal slips quietly through the outskirts of Stafford. The county town stood an aloof mile to the west of the Staffs & Worcs Canal which, in true Brindley fashion, followed the easy contours of the Penk Valley. Plans to construct a branch were dropped in favour of a simple lock down into the Sow, the river being dredged and realigned to take boats as far as a terminal basin at Green Bridge in the centre of Stafford. The navigation was opened in 1816 and in use until the end of the First World War. A footpath follows the riverbank into the town, but it is difficult to envisage how seventy foot narrowboats ever got up there. A group known as Stafford Riverway Link has been formed to promote restoration of this long lost route as a boost to the county town's economy.

Baswich church once stood as isolated on its hillside as Acton Trussell's does still, but now it is surrounded by a housing development, though those with an interest in ecclesiastical architecture can easily reach it from Bridge 100. Note the spelling of the village's name with a 'k' on the bridgeplate. There was a substantial wharf by Radford Bridge, but its site is now somewhat less interestingly occupied by a car showroom following demolition of the original warehouses in the Philistine seventies.

Stafford Boat Club - with their impressive club house and welcome to visiting boaters - occupy a former brickworks arm near Hazelstrine

Bridge. Most of the works' output was despatched by canal. Bridge 97 has disappeared completely, there being not even any tell-tale narrowing in the canal's channel where it once must have stood.

Radford Meadows form part of the River Penk's floodplain and are now administered by the Staffordshire Wildlife Trust as a nature reserve. Public access is restricted to special events, but the towpath offers fine views (and interpretive boards) of what is nowadays quite a rare environment. Radford's signature species is the rare Black Poplar tree. Snipe, which in the past would have bred here in significant numbers, are also being encouraged to return.

The lock-keeper's cottage at Deptmore had been, throughout most of the life of the *Canal Companions*, the home of a reclusive character, whose only means of contact with the outside world had been by means of a motorised pontoon which was kept in an off-side lay-by at the tail of the lock. Now, following a period of abandonment, a track has been forged through the fields and the house is being renovated.

Acton Trussell - which you'd expect with such a name to be a picture book English village - fails to live up to expectations with its banal modern architecture. The solitary building on the towpath side used to be a boatman's pub. Present day boaters, however, slake their thirst in the old moated house by Bridge 92, now well-established as a bar, restaurant and hotel set in charming grounds. It is said that Brindley actually used the old house's moat for a few yards when building the canal: anything to save a few bob.

AS the canal ascends to (or descends from) its summit level, the locks come thick and fast. The motorway retreats, only to be replaced by the housing estates which cling-wrap the essentially agreeable little town of Penkridge. Yet, a mile on either side, the countryside is characterised by rolling farmland lifting to the bulwark of Cannock Chase.

The towpath between bridges 90 and 86 is hi-jacked by the "Staffordshire Way" which seems forever to be bumping into canals and appropriating towpaths in the course of its 92 mile journey from Mow Cop to Kinver Edge. Its route has come down off The Chase and crossed Teddesley Park. Teddesley Hall was the seat of Sir Edward Littleton, one of the chief promoters of the Staffordshire & Worcestershire Canal. Indeed, the family remained involved with the canal company until its nationalisation in 1947. The hall itself was demolished by the army in the mid Fifties (having been used as a prison camp for German officers during the Second World War) but the estate farm remains, hidden from the canal by some woodland known as Wellington Belt in commemoration of a visit to the hall by the Iron Duke. Bridge 89 once had ornate balustrades commensurate with its importance as the gateway to the hall, but, irresponsibly and unforgivably, these have been infilled by ugly brickwork.

Rather sadly, the Teddesley Boat Company has ceased offering boats for hire. One by one these family firms, who were at the forefront of the hiring boom which hit the canals in the nineteen-seventies, are ceasing to operate or being taken over, and the canal scene is somehow poorer for their passing.

Many boaters pause to take on water at Penkridge Wharf, but there is usually room to moor up for a visit to the town. The Littletons had fingers in many pies, not least the local colliery, which at one time employed over a thousand men. A huge basin, now covered by the motorway, was constructed to enable boats to be loaded with coal from a raised pier by gravity. The chief traffic flow of Littleton coal by canal in later years was down

to Stourport Power Station. The mine closed in 1993. Rodbaston Lock had a keeper until the motorway was built. A special bridge was built over the new road to maintain access to his lockside cottage, but the noise of the ensuing traffic was so bad as to cause him to leave and find new accommodation, the cottage subsequently being demolished. West of the canal between Otherton and Rodbaston lies a college of agriculture.

Rodbaston 80
former colliery basin
31
35 Rodbaston Lock 8ft 6ins
Otherton Lane 81
80A Littleton Coly Rly
Otherton 82
Otherton 36 Lock 10ft 3ins
Otherton Boat Haven
course of former colliery railway
Lynehill 83
Penkridge Lock 9ft 3ins
84 83A
Longford Lock 10ft 0ins
37
70'
Cross Keys
86 85 Filance Lock 10ft 3ins
87A 87
38
A449
WOLVERHAMPTON
Staffs Way
39 Boat
Penkridge
88A
Teddesley Park 89
sch
Co-op
88 Longford
River Penk
mill
market
Teddesley Boat Co. Midland Chandlers Park Gate 90
Staffs Way
for details of facilities at Penkridge turn back to page 62
viaduct
STAFFORD
SW
by-road to Brewood
P
40 Park Gate Lock 7ft 6ins
Shutt Hill Lock 6ft 0ins
41 Shutt Hill 91
M6 Northbound
29

31 STAFFS & WORCS CANAL Gailey & Hatherton 3mls/3lks/2hrs

CALF HEATH is a strangely isolated tract of country, pancake flat and crossed by a grid of sullen little roads, with here and there a huddle of houses, gathered reassuringly together like something out of Van Gogh's early potato field paintings. The canal all but boxes the compass of this gravel pit-riddled landscape, so that The Chase with its communications tower and the chemical works with its phalanx of flaring chimneys, appear to move about you, teasing you into geographic insecurity, like a game of Blind Man's Buff.

The Staffs & Worcs Canal's summit - from Gailey to Compton - lies at more or less 340 feet above sea level. If you've climbed up from Penkridge and beyond it's a relief to be done with locks for the time being. Industry lines the canal at Four Ashes. A former tar works here was once served by Thomas Clayton boats.

The last load of Cannock coal came off the Hatherton Branch in 1949 and it was abandoned a couple of years later. However, the illusion of a junction remains, because the bottom lock (of what was once a flight of eight in three miles) is still used to provide access to moorings. The Lichfield and Hatherton Canals Restoration Trust is actively seeking restoration of the branch with the intention of linking it with the northern waters of the BCN at Norton Canes, and there is little doubt that its opening would prove a great fillip to the under-boated northern extremities of the BCN.

Watling Street crosses the canal at Gailey. The most significant feature here is the 'round house', originally a toll clerk's office but now a splendid canal shop run by mother and daughter team, Eileen and Karen Lester; the former a keen Wolves supporter, the latter favouring Villa. There is something spell-binding about cylindrical buildings - Martello towers, windmills, lighthouses; even Birmingham's Bull Ring Rotunda - and Gailey roundhouse, in its lock-side setting, has a particular charm which begs to be captured on camera.

A5 to London

course of Hatherton Branch

Gailey Reservoirs

Hatherton Junction

Calf Heath

70'

70'

32

Long Moll's 76

Deepmore 75

M6

Calf Heath Reservoir

30

Boggs Lock 8ft 6ins

34

Brick Kiln Lock 8ft 6ins

33

79

32

Roundhouse Canal Shop

Gailey Wharf

A5 Watling Street

Gailey Lock 8ft 6ins

ABC Boat Hire J. D. Boat Services

canoeing !

Four Ashes

70'

Calf Heath **77** *industrial estate*

chemical works

78

78A

Four Ashes (csd 1959)

Stafford - Wolverhampton

Gailey (csd 1951)

✗ *nursery*

Pottery

Dobbies Garden World

A449

Summary of Facilities
A short walk westwards along the A5 will take you (past a nursery with tea room) to Gailey roundabout and a number of potential attractions: a small general store; a pottery housed in a former church; a large Marston's pub called the Spread Eagle; and Dobbies Garden World. Arriva bus 76 runs hourly to Penkridge and Wolverhampton.

32 STAFFS & WORCS CANAL Coven 4mls/0lks/1.5hrs

THE world is divided - though not perhaps equally - into those of who think of The Laches as Plato's Socratic dialogue on the nature of courage, and those who think of it as a bridge on the Staffordshire & Worcestershire Canal. Knowing full well which category it falls into, the canal imperviously exchanges the loneliness of Calf and Coven heaths for the industrial and suburban outskirts of Wolverhampton; the M54 to Telford forming an obvious, though not intentional, boundary.

At Cross Green a former boatman's pub called "The Anchor" has transmogrified into the "Fox & Anchor", a popular restaurant bar, and many boaters choose to moor here overnight. Skirting a golfing centre, followed by a sewage works, the canal passes beneath the M54 and crosses the county boundary between Staffordshire and the West Midlands, one of those nebulous new counties which had its origins in the local government changes of 1974. To the west of the canal the new 'i-54' high tech

business park continues to attract inward investment and blue chip manufacturers such as Jaguar Landrover. Employees use the towpath as a short cut to Morrisons for their take-away lunches.

The most significant feature of this length is "Pendeford Rockin", the old boatmen's name for a shallow, but tellingly narrow cutting hewn by Brindley's navvies through a solid belt of sandstone which breaks through the clay strata at this point. The cutting, half a mile or so long, restricts the channel to such a degree that you begin to wonder if you have lost concentration and taken a wrong turn. There are, however, one or two passing places - as on a single lane road - where oncoming boats can be successfully negotiated without losing one's temper. As the canal moves towards Autherley Junction it skirts the perimeter of a large school, screened from the waterway by an intimidating line of Lombardy poplars which have the look of teachers sternly trying to keep order at Assembly.

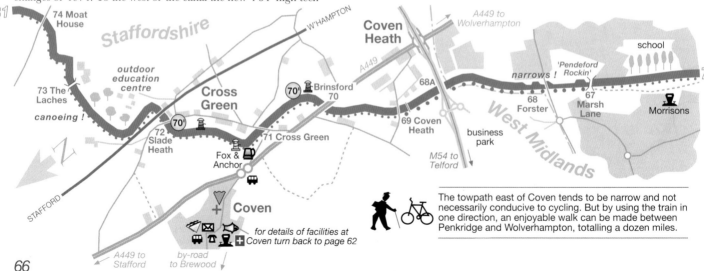

The towpath east of Coven tends to be narrow and not necessarily conducive to cycling. But by using the train in one direction, an enjoyable walk can be made between Penkridge and Wolverhampton, totalling a dozen miles.

for details of facilities at Coven turn back to page 62

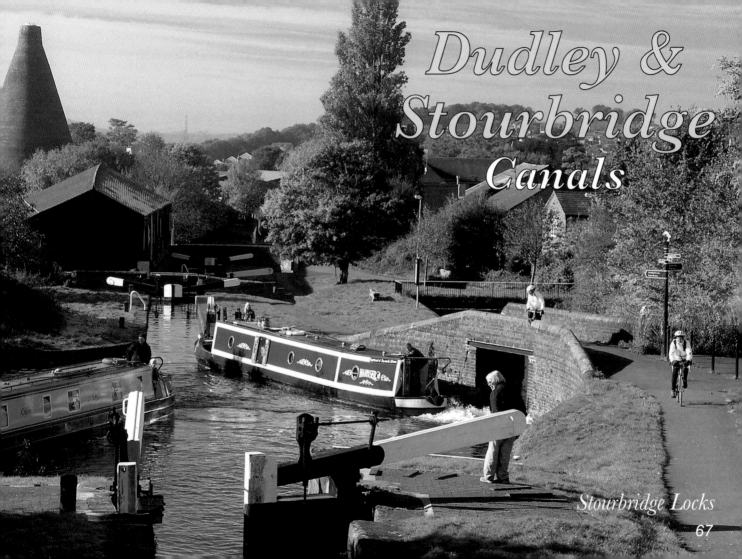

Dudley & Stourbridge Canals

Stourbridge Locks

33 STOURBRIDGE CANAL Stourton-Black Delph 5mls/20lks/6hrs

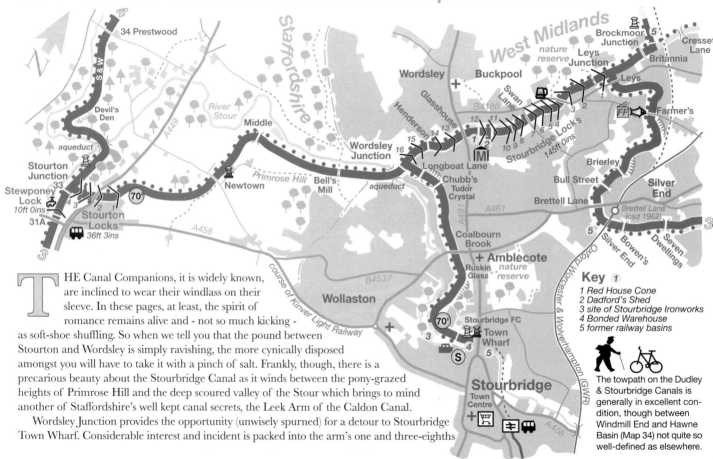

Key 1
1 Red House Cone
2 Dadford's Shed
3 site of Stourbridge Ironworks
4 Bonded Warehouse
5 former railway basins

The towpath on the Dudley & Stourbridge Canals is generally in excellent condition, though between Windmill End and Hawne Basin (Map 34) not quite so well-defined as elsewhere.

THE Canal Companions, it is widely known, are inclined to wear their windlass on their sleeve. In these pages, at least, the spirit of romance remains alive and - not so much kicking - as soft-shoe shuffling. So when we tell you that the pound between Stourton and Wordsley is simply ravishing, the more cynically disposed amongst you will have to take it with a pinch of salt. Frankly, though, there is a precarious beauty about the Stourbridge Canal as it winds between the pony-grazed heights of Primrose Hill and the deep scoured valley of the Stour which brings to mind another of Staffordshire's well kept canal secrets, the Leek Arm of the Caldon Canal.

Wordsley Junction provides the opportunity (unwisely spurned) for a detour to Stourbridge Town Wharf. Considerable interest and incident is packed into the arm's one and three-eighths of a mile length: the old Dial glassworks by Chubbs Bridge (where a visit can be made to the Tudor Crystal Factory shop); Coalbourn Brook Bridge which used to carry the Kinver Light Railway (where a visit can be made to Ruskin Glass); and the remains of Stourbridge Iron Works where the first steam locomotive to operate in the USA was built. Named *Stourbridge Lion*, it puffed its way through Pennsylvania in 1829. The works had been founded by John Bradley in 1798. His name appears on the southernmost roving bridge, a diminutive structure of cast iron construction dated 1873.

The arm terminates felicitously enough at the foot of Stourbridge High Street (though it formerly proceeded a short distance beyond to a railway transhipment basin) beside a handsomely restored bonded warehouse where secure visitor moorings, along with lavish boating facilities (pump-out, Elsan, water, gas, coal, canalia etc) are provided by the Stourbridge Navigation Trust.

The Stourbridge Sixteen

The flight is characterised by reedy side ponds aiding and abetting water supply. Furthermore it is accompanied by the spirits of the long deceased industries - coal, clay and iron - whose trade made it so prosperous in its heyday. Most of the evidence of these trades is confined to old maps, but two classic survivors remain in the form of "Dadford's Shed", a former transhipment warehouse built of timber and now partially used by a boatbuilder; and the massive Red House Cone (or kiln) which dates from

the end of the 18th Century and which is now incorporated into a glass-making heritage centre. Locks 9 and 10 are telescoped together like a mini-Bratch, and were similarly once a true staircase. The Bottle & Glass, which used to stand by Lock 3, now resides in the Black Country Living Museum.

Leys Junction - Black Delph

Leys Junction may not be much to look at now, but it is effectively the custom post to the lost worlds of the Fens Branch and Stourbridge Extension Canal. The SEC was opened in 1840, enjoying six brief years of independence before being absorbed by the Oxford, Worcester & Wolverhampton Railway. Its goal was the coal and ironstone deposits at Shut End, two miles to the north-west. Navigation is feasible as far as Brockmoor, where secure offside visitor moorings have been installed. But the setting is lugubrious to say the least, and one imagines that walkers will derive most pleasure from exploring these forgotten routes.

The main line veers east, essaying a serpentine course through housing zones and echoes of industry past and present. Hereabouts - as we remarked in an earlier edition - realisation comes suddenly that you are no longer a holidaymaker, but rather a traveller in the strictest sense of the term, as adventurously off the beaten track as if you were mountain-busting in darkest Peru. At Black Delph Junction the Stourbridge Canal makes an unheralded and imperceptible end-on junction with the Dudley No.1 Canal, and the next part of your journey is covered by Map 34.

Stourbridge
Map 33

From the canal wharf, it's but a short walk through the underpass beneath the ring-road (which encircles the glass-making town of Stourbridge like a boa-constrictor) to the town centre. And how unexpected! For Stourbridge is not yet another Black Country throwback, but an independent market town with a profusion of shops and some not uninteresting architecture. Ascending Lower High Street one's eyes are drawn firstly to the elegant town house 'Stourhurst', secondly the Unitarian Chapel of 1788 and thirdly to the former Grammar School which even

Nikolaus Pevsner (Teutonically predisposed to understatement) was moved to label 'picturesque'. At the top of the climb stands the town clock; imposing, fluted-columned, cast in the local iron works in 1857, and equipped with a match-striking plate (a typical piece of Victorian ingenuity) for passers by.

Eating & Drinking

CELLARS - High Street. Tel: 01384 444829. Indian restaurant within easy reach of the basin. DY8 1TT
FRENCH CONNECTION - Coventry Street (opposite the town clock). Tel: 01384 390940. French cooking in the Black Country is rather rare and this

little bistro is, *heureusement*, an exception. DY8 1EP
ROYAL EXCHANGE - Enville Street. Tel: 01384 396726. Batham's tied house offering only cobs and pork pies to support the serious business of downing this wonderful Black Country brew. DY8 1EX
Real ale enthusiasts should also seek out the DUKE WILLIAM on Coventry Street.
SAMSON & LION - canalside Lock 4 of Stourbridge flight. Tel: 01384 77796. Banks's and Marston's beers, good food and a friendly atmosphere. Skittle alley and garden with aviary. Accommodation. DY8 5SP
A Chinese takeaway abuts the basin - Tel: 01384 396730.
continued overleaf:

continued from page 69:

Shopping

Redevelopment of the Crown Centre has brought a large new Tesco supermarket right into the town centre, but the town's independent retailers still appear to flourish. Three favourites are Nickolls & Perks (established 1797) wine merchants at the top of Lower High Street; the French Delicatessen on Coventry Street which offers a mouthwatering selection of meats and regional cheeses as well as freshly made and incredibly inexpensive take-away baguettes and paninis; and Ocean Seafood on Market Street: nice to see a fishmonger in this landlocked part of the world.

Things to Do

RED HOUSE GLASS CONE - adjacent Lock 12 of Stourbridge flight. Tel: 01384 812750. Self guided audio tours, including ascent of spiral staircase within the vertigo-inducing hundred foot high cone itself. Crafts, gifts, refreshments etc. Open daily, free admission, offside moorings for boating visitors. DY8 4AZ Other glass makers include Tudor Crystal (Tel: 01384 392525) and Ruskin (Tel: 01384 399419). STOURBRIDGE NAVIGATION TRUST - Canal Street. Tel: 01384 395216. Administrators of town wharf and bonded warehouse. Warm welcome, 'bostin' facilities. DY8 4LU

Connections

BUSES - services throughout the area from bus station at top of High Street. Hansons services 227/8 run hourly Mon-Sat to/from Kinver via Stewponey. *Though surely such an attractive 'tourist' destination deserves a Sunday service!* Tel: 0871 200 2233.

TRAINS - shuttle service aboard pod-like 'people-movers' on Britain's shortest branch line between Stourbridge Town and Stourbridge Junction for connections to Birmingham and Worcester. One of the world's great *little* railway journeys.
Tel: 03457 484950.

TAXIS - Falcon Taxis. Tel: 01384 393939.

Merry Hill　　　　　　　Map 34

Of course (what they now call *intu*) Merry Hill is really Brierley Hill, but so much does the massive retail complex dominate the vicinity now, that it seems more appropriate to refer to it thus. In common with its peers - Meadowhall, Metro, Trafford Park and Bluewater - you either love this sort of thing or loathe it. "Over 200 shops and stores" shrieks the publicity blurb: "two and a half miles of marbled halls - a uniquely enjoyable experience" - much like the BCN itself you might justifiably retort!

Eating & Drinking

The Waterfront features a Wetherspoons and a Marston's pub, but real ale enthusiasts will want to visit: THE VINE - Delph Road. Tel: 01384 78293. Better known as the 'Bull & Bladder', Batham's brewery tap is one of the great Black Country pubs. It stands on Delph Road about six minutes walk east from the foot of Delph Locks. Food available at lunchtime on weekdays, and Batham's ambrosial beer which the family have been brewing for five generations. The Vine, one of only ten tied houses, has a Shakespearean quotation emblazoned across its frontage at roof level. DY5 2TN

Shopping

If the prospect of Merry Hill's two hundred plus shops is more than you can bear, then head in the opposite direction for Brierley Hill's beleaguered but traditional High Street. Note also the existence of a Odeon multi-screen cinema complex adjacent to the canal south of Green's Bridge: there's sure to be some twaddle on.

Connections

BUSES - will take you back to reality with a - "did I *really* spend all that" - bump. Tel: 0871 200 2233.
TAXIS - Newline Taxis. Tel: 01384 480001.

Netherton　　　　　　　Map 34

Netherton was literally and metaphorically built on coal. The parish church of St Andrew's stands 600ft above sea level on a bare hillside once extensively mined. From its summit there are views across the intervening valley, traversed by the Dudley Canal, to Brierley Hill and the distant horizon of The Wrekin. The sturdy church itself, surrounded by tombstones which tell their own Black Country story of industrial triumph and personal misery, was locked, but we could see that it contained a gallery supported by cast iron columns as well as some interesting stained glass. Noah Hingley's memorial may be found in the graveyard.

Eating & Drinking

THE OLDE SWAN - Halesowen Road. Tel: 01384 253075). Older regulars still lovingly call it 'Ma Pardoe's' after a former landlady. They brew on the premises and a lovely pale, fruity beer the bitter is too. Additionally a wide choice of food is available lunchtimes and evenings. DY2 9PY

Shopping

It must be hard being an independent shop-keeper in the all-pervading thrall of Merry Hill, but Netherton's shops evince character and courtesy with Black Country wit never far from the surface. Flavells butchers sell home made pies at the top of Cradley Road, whilst Allans discount store remains an essential point of pilgrimage: 'every seasonable line imaginable - no nonsense prices'. Meanwhile, no self-respecting cowpoke would miss the chance to visit the Ranch House Western Store - 'complete Western & Line Dance outfitters'. Bain's Wines offer a good range of bottled beer, not least Bathams. There are Lidl and Aldi supermarkets; convenience stores, pharmacies, a post office and a Lloyds Bank.

Things to Do

BUMBLE HOLE VISITOR CENTRE - Tel: 01384 814100. Interesting and friendly centre devoted to Windmill End and its post-industrial environs.

Connections

BUSES - frequent services to/from Dudley etc. Nearest railway station at Old Hill. Tel: 0871 200 2233.

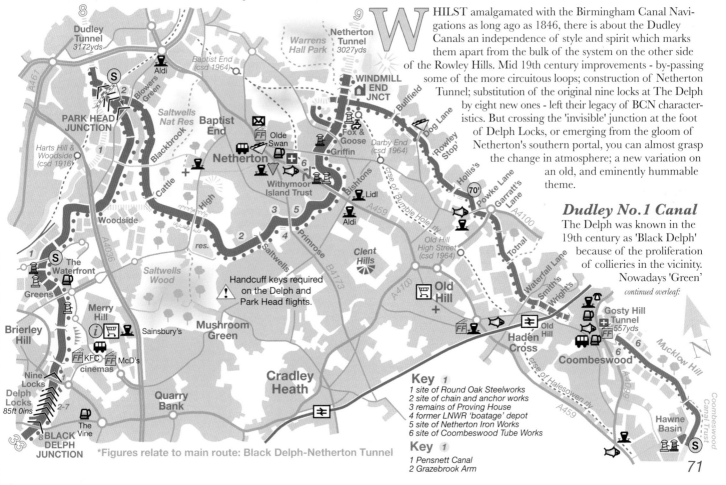

WHILST amalgamated with the Birmingham Canal Navigations as long ago as 1846, there is about the Dudley Canals an independence of style and spirit which marks them apart from the bulk of the system on the other side of the Rowley Hills. Mid 19th century improvements - by-passing some of the more circuitous loops; construction of Netherton Tunnel; substitution of the original nine locks at The Delph by eight new ones - left their legacy of BCN characteristics. But crossing the 'invisible' junction at the foot of Delph Locks, or emerging from the gloom of Netherton's southern portal, you can almost grasp the change in atmosphere; a new variation on an old, and eminently hummable theme.

Dudley No.1 Canal

The Delph was known in the 19th century as 'Black Delph' because of the proliferation of collieries in the vicinity. Nowadays 'Green'

continued overleaf:

continued overleaf:

Map labels:

Dudley Tunnel 3172yds
Warrens Hall Park
Netherton Tunnel 3027yds
Baptist End (csd 1964)
Aldi
Blowers Green
PARK HEAD JUNCTION
Saltwells Nat Res
Baptist End
Blackbrook
Netherton
Olde Swan
Fox & Goose
Griffin
Darby End (csd 1964)
WINDMILL END JNCT
Bullfield
Dog Lane
'Rowley Stop'
Hollis's
Harts Hill & Woodside (csd 1916)
Cattle
High
Withymoor Island Trust
Bishtons
Lidl
Aldi
'Course of Bumble Hole' rly
70'
Powke Lane
Garratt's Lane
Woodside
res.
Saltwells
Primrose
Clent Hills
Old Hill High Street (csd 1964)
Totnal
Waterfall Lane
Smith's
Wright's
The Waterfront
Greens
Saltwells Wood
Handcuff keys required on the Delph and Park Head flights.
Old Hill
Haden Cross
Old Hill
Gosty Hill Tunnel 557yds
Mucklow Hill
Merry Hill
Sainsbury's
Mushroom Green
Coombeswood
N
Brierley Hill
KFC
McD's
cinemas
Cradley Heath
Coombeswood Canal Trust
Nine Locks
Delph Locks 85ft 0ins
The Vine
Quarry Bank
Hawne Basin
BLACK DELPH JUNCTION

Key 1
1 site of Round Oak Steelworks
2 site of chain and anchor works
3 remains of Proving House
4 former LNWR 'boatage' depot
5 site of Netherton Iron Works
6 site of Coombeswood Tube Works

Key 1
1 Pensnett Canal
2 Grazebrook Arm

*Figures relate to main route: Black Delph-Netherton Tunnel

The Waterfront

WATERFRONT WAY

🔥🍴☕🗑 WC

Round Oak
Bridge 1

☎ ✉
Lord Dudley's
Bridge

📱 Wetherspoons
New Level
Furnace Bridge

📱 Brewer's
Wharf

LEVEL STREET

Green's
Bridge

N

continued from page 71:

would be a more appropriate sobriquet, for barely a vestige of industry remains. Delph Locks consist of eight chambers, of which six are in close proximity, carrying the canal from the 356ft level of the Stourbridge Canal to the 441ft contour of the Dudley No.1 Canal. The flight is one of the most spectacular anywhere on the canal system, but because of its location on the esoteric BCN it tends to be less celebrated than the likes of Bingley, Foxton and Devizes. On the off-side of the locks a series of overflow weirs cascade spectacularly when water levels are high. When the canal opened in 1779 there were nine locks. The top and bottom are originals, but in 1858 the present central six were built to replace seven earlier locks, traces of which can be explored to the east. A Horseley Iron Works roving bridge spans the original course of the canal below the top lock. In the middle of the flight a former block of canal horse stables is leased to the BCN Society and is occasionally open to the public.

Having acclimatized yourself to the 19th century environs of Black Delph, the next bend in the canal opens out to reveal the 21st century vista of Merry Hill, one of the out of town shopping developments akin to Sheffield's Meadowhall or the Metro Centre at Gateshead which we gladly seem to have grown out of. The canal has recently been slightly rerouted and one benefit of this work is the provision of mooring rings for boaters intending to moor up and visit the centre; though many of you will doubtless have taken to the water to escape such manifestations of modern life.

The Waterfront, a billion pound development mixing commerce with leisure, occupies the site of the once vast Round Oak steel works. Aesthetically it is barely an improvement on the past: arguably the most satisfying building of the development is the pub, a pastiched cross between an East Anglian watermill and a Black Country foundry with plenty of mock weatherboarding and reconditioned brick; there must be a moral in that somewhere. Pre-book pontoon 'pay moorings' with electricity and water laid on are available if you're so inclined, a facility more likely to appeal to private boaters rather than hirers - telephone 01384 487911/2 for further details.

Passing the former junction of the Two Locks Line at Woodside Junction, the canal reaches the 12 feet deep Blower's Green Lock and Park Head Junction. Here the two Dudley Canals met, the No.1 Canal proceeding up the Park Head flight to the portal of Dudley Tunnel. The Dudley Canal Trust provide a tug service to haul boats through their Aladdin's Cave of a tunnel; though stringent size limitations apply. The Trust can be contacted (Tel: 0121 557 6265 - *www.dudleycanaltrust.org.uk*) for advice and further details, and the more advance warning they get of your intended passage the better. It is rewarding, however, to visit Park Head, if only to admire the handsome pump house - which the Trust have developed as an educational centre - and to take in the canal scene as a whole, and we can recommend mooring here and strolling up to view, not only the southern portal of Dudley Tunnel, but the interesting remains of the Pensnett Canal and Grazebrook Arm as well.

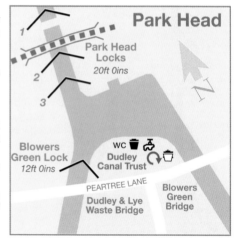

Park Head

1

Park Head
Locks
20ft 0ins

2

3

N

Blowers
Green Lock
12ft 0ins

WC 🗑 🚲
Dudley
Canal Trust

PEARTREE LANE

Dudley & Lye
Waste Bridge

Blowers
Green
Bridge

Park Head - Windmill End

The Dudley No.2 Canal once totalled eleven route miles, linking the Dudley No.1 Canal at Park Head with the Worcester & Birmingham Canal at Selly Oak (Map 11). It was completed in 1798 and included Britain's fourth longest canal tunnel at Lapal (3795 yards), a daunting towpath-less bore subject to a unique system of operation whereby a steam pumping engine produced an artificial bi-directional current through the tunnel to aid the momentum of boats passing through.

Between Park Head and Windmill End the canal describes a wide arc, clinging to the 453ft contour at the foot of Netherton Hill. Once upon a time industry congregated beside its banks: collieries, claypits, furnaces, limekilns and ironworks. But now this is coot country and the reeds seem as abundant as any Broadland river. At Blackbrook Junction the other end of the Two Locks Line is still evident through its roving bridge, even if subsidence caused it to be abandoned in 1909. Clothed in gorse and hawthorn, Netherton Hill stands behind the erstwhile junction, climbing to a 600ft summit topped by St Andrew's church where cholera victims are buried in unmarked common graves in the churchyard. The surrounding environs offer generous views over the southern extents of the not so Black Country and the distant wooded tops of the Clent Hills rising to a thousand feet southwards beyond Halesowen.

A housing estate occupies the site of Doulton's once extensive clay pit linked to the canal by a tramway incline. Boats would carry this clay along the Dudley Canal to the firm's works at Darby End. High Bridge spans a rocky cutting where originally the canal builders built a short-lived tunnel. Nowadays the exhaust from your boat reverberates and rebounds between the sheer sandstone slopes of the cutting. No wonder the old boatmen nicknamed this 'Sounding Bridge'. Lodge Farm reservoir, used for watersports, gleams like antimony in its cup of land between the canal and Saltwells Nature Reserve. Footpaths penetrate its jungle, threading their way through alligator-haunted swamps down to Cradley Heath.

We have seen elsewhere on the BCN how the railways developed a network of interchange basins and boatage depots. Two examples of this are encountered hereabouts. Primrose Boatage Depot provided the LMS Railway (and its antecedents) with water access to an area otherwise dominated by GWR lines. LMS boats traded between here and the company's interchange basins at Bloomfield (Map 8) and Albion (Map 9). Half a mile away, by Bishtons Bridge, the Great Western Railway's Withymoor Basin was one of the most extensive interchange points between rail and canal in its heyday. Withymoor opened in 1878 and closed in 1965. Its last regular transhipment cargo was chain from Lloyds Proving House by Primrose Bridge. Sadly its transhipment sheds and canopies have been demolished, but its arm survives in water, providing useful boating facilities (including pump-out) and residential moorings for the Withymoor Island Trust.

Mention of chain recalls Netherton's landbased involvement in maritime engineering. Did you know that the *Titanic's* anchors were cast here? Each anchor required a team of twenty-four horses to tow it out of Netherton. There was a tradition of chain and anchor making in this unlikely corner of the Black Country. Much of the chain-making was done by women packed tightly in small premises which became so hot that they habitually worked bare-breasted. Would that the Black Country had had an artist of the calibre of Joseph Wright of Derby to do justice to such scenes. The workshops of the new estates which fringe the canal seem nebulous in comparison. Hingley's, owners of Netherton Ironworks, were instrumental in the establishment of Midlands & Coast Canal Carriers following the demise of the Shropshire Union fleet in 1921.

Windmill End is arguably the epitome of the Black Country canal scene, and given its location at the centre of the inland waterways system, together with the public open space which lines its canal banks, it's not surprising that it serves from time to time as an ideal venue for major boat rallies. The gaunt outline of Cobb's engine house, silhouetted against the Rowley Hills, above a profusion of Toll End Works roving bridges, forms one of the Black Country's most potent post-industrial images. If only the 'Bumble Hole' push & pull train still steamed back and forth between Dudley and Old Hill. Windmill End station was immortalised in Flanders & Swann's haunting elegy *Slow Train*. On Christmas Eve 1914 - when, goodness knows, there was already enough suffering in the world - three young people drowned in the canal, having apparently lost their way in darkness, snow and fog between the railway station and their homes.

continued on page 76:

TOP LOCK BRIDGE

1 Wordsley
2 The Delph
3 Brierley Hill Bull Terrier
4 Park Head Pastoral

1 Woodside
2 Stourbridge
3 Stourton Junction
4 Windmill End
5 Netherton Tunnel

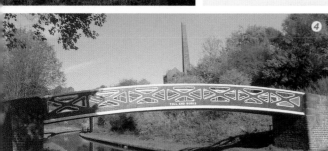

continued from page 73:

Cobb's engine house contained a stationary steam engine which pumped excess water from coal mines in the vicinity and discharged it into the canal. Built in 1831, the engine kept the pits dry and the cut wet for well nigh a century, until the local collieries were all worked out. The engine subsequently went for scrap, but the engine house remains, adorning the landscape as if somehow transmuted from a Cornish cliff top. The old colliery precincts surrounding Windmill End are now known as Warren's Hall Park; a haunted countryside to saunter in, to go roaming in the gloaming in, imagining the pandemonium of its industrial past.

Three cast iron roving bridges span the waterways radiating from Windmill End Junction. Originally the Dudley No.2 Canal ran east to west here, following the course of what became quaintly known as the 'Boshboil' and 'Bumble Hole' arms after the loop was cut off by the improvements of 1858 associated with the opening of Netherton Tunnel. The tunnel's southern portal stands to the north of the junction through the arch of a blue-brick overbridge which carried a colliery tramway.

Netherton Tunnel provokes piquant contrast with Dudley Tunnel's ancient confines. High, wide and equipped with twin towpaths, it now lacks only the lighting once generated by a turbine fed from the high level old main line at Tividale (Map 9). It takes roughly half an hour to walk (advisably with a torch) or boat through this monument to the last fling of the canal age. We counted seven airshafts providing 'air-raids' of rainwater, but we've met wetter tunnels on our canal travels.

Windmill End - Hawne Basin

Lapal Tunnel's closure in 1917 severed the Dudley No.2 Canal's route between Windmill End and Selly Oak, but this end of the canal remained in commercial use right up until 1969 to serve the giant Stewart & Lloyds tube making works at Coombeswood on the far side of Gosty Hill Tunnel. Thereafter the canal might easily have deteriorated but for the emergence of the Coombeswood Canal Trust who developed the railway interchange basin at Hawne, on the outskirts of Halesowen, into a flourishing centre of Black Country leisure boating. The journey down to Hawne is continually engrossing if less than edifying. Old basins abound and 19th century large scale maps illuminate the density of industry here. The canal still narrows

at Rowley Stop, but these days no one materialises to take the tolls, so you proceed beneath Hollis's Bridge and on past a roving bridge under which an arm once extended into Old Hill Ironworks. Opposite here, we were gratified to learn, stood Pearson's Colliery, but if we were counting on the shares as part of our inheritance, we were in for a disappointment.

By Powke Lane stands the substantial Rowley Regis crematorium and cemetery and suburban Blackheath occupies the adjacent hillside. At Old Hill a series of overbridges pass in quick succession as the canal approaches the stygian delights of Gosty Hill Tunnel. In the early years of the 20th century the BCN operated a tug service through the tunnel and the remains of its dock can be seen beside the northern portal. The tunnel's confined, towpathless bore is infamous in boating circles. Working boatmen were content to abandon the tiller and spend the time it took to pass through the 557 yards long tunnel in their boat cabins, whilst, as snugly as a piston in a cylinder, the boat made its own way from one end to another.

You used to emerge from Gosty Hill Tunnel into the eerie precincts of the tube works. The canal traversed a canyon of sheer brick walls and passed beneath a sequence of mysterious corrugated iron clad overbridges and pipes whispering sibilantly with escaping steam. All this has vanished and been redeveloped into a trading estate of soulless units, inscrutable behind their ubiquitous cladding and characterless trading names, though we did uncover the fact that Arcelor Mittal is the world's largest steel producer with its headquarters in Luxembourg, a far cry from the comparative parochiality of Stewart & Lloyds. Beyond such interlopers, the canal runs at the foot of Mucklow Hill, a pleasant open landscape threaded by public footpaths, before abruptly reaching the old transhipment basin at Hawne, loomed over by a huge B&Q. Visiting boaters are welcomed (there is an excellent range of facilities, including laundry and showers) and this is definitely one Black Country mooring where the spectre of vandalism won't disturb your slumbers. The preserved working pair of narrowboats *Atlas* and *Malus* are based here. As to the remainder of the Dudley No.2's route, its future lies in the enthusiastic hands of the Lapal Canal Trust.

B.C.N.
backwaters

MEANDERING in the best tradition of a contour canal, the Wyrley & Essington lives up to its nickname - "Curly Wyrley". It opened, independently of the Birmingham Canal, in 1797; extending for 24 miles from Horseley Fields, Wolverhampton to Huddlesford Junction on the Coventry Canal (Map 24) near Lichfield. Its fidelity to the 473ft contour was absolute until Ogley (Map 37) beyond which there were no less than thirty locks in the seven mile stretch down to Huddlesford. Several branches were built, so that by the mid 19th century there were half a dozen or more important junctions adding traffic to what had become a route of much importance. The W&E merged with the BCN in 1840.

After the disappearance of trade from this canal, it fell into neglect. Technically it remained navigable, but it was too ugly to appeal to all but the most hardened and perverse of pleasure boaters. And to all intents and purposes, despite the march of redevelopment along its banks, together with a general mellowing in atmosphere, the 'Curly Wyrley' remains an unloved canal, and one rarely boated.

Leaving the outskirts of Wolverhampton astern, at Horseley Fields' lugubrious junction, the W&E takes little trouble with its appearance as it heads towards Wednesfield. At Heath Town an aqueduct carries it across the Grand Junction Railway, forty years its junior. Blue brick abutments recall the existence of the Midland Railway's line between Wolverhampton and Walsall, abandoned - as far as passengers were concerned - upon the inauguration of a trolleybus service between the two towns in 1931, though the local station had already ceased functioning, doubtless rendered obsolete by the trams which predated the trolleybuses.

Apart from a truncated arm which somewhat vainly offers visitor moorings, all trace of the Bentley Canal (which linked the W&E with the Walsall Canal at Darlaston (Map 41) has vanished under a retail park. Wednesfield turns its back on the canal but offers vestiges of civilisation. At Lane Head the arm which served Holly Bank Colliery basin is still in water, though no longer do the mineral trains come clangorously down from Hilton Main.

Map

Heath Town (csd 1910)

Wednesfield Junction

New Cross

New Bentley

Church

Pintold

Rookery

WC Town Centre

Wednesfield

Sainsbury's

cinemas FF

Jolly Collier

Deans Road

Heath Town

Grand Junction Railway

A4124

HORSELEY FIELDS JUNCTION

7

1

2

Moat House

Devils Elbow

Wards

Olinthus

3

Castle

A4124

A462

Perry Hall

Pool Hayes

Knights

New Invention

4

Lane Head

Adam & Eve

FF

course of Midland Railway Wolverhampton-Walsall

Bentley Canal

N

Key 1

1 rems of Midland Railway boat dock
2 site of Midland Railway basins
3 site of colliery basin
4 Holly Bank Colliery basin

for details of facilities at Wednesfield and Lane Head turn to page 81

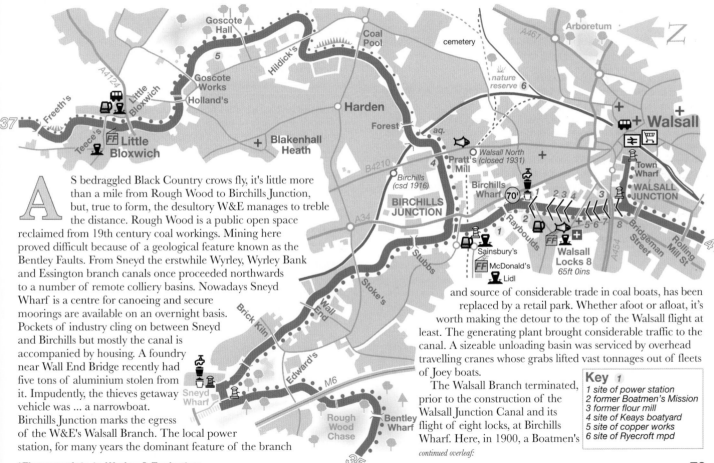

AS bedraggled Black Country crows fly, it's little more than a mile from Rough Wood to Birchills Junction, but, true to form, the desultory W&E manages to treble the distance. Rough Wood is a public open space reclaimed from 19th century coal workings. Mining here proved difficult because of a geological feature known as the Bentley Faults. From Sneyd the erstwhile Wyrley, Wyrley Bank and Essington branch canals once proceeded northwards to a number of remote colliery basins. Nowadays Sneyd Wharf is a centre for canoeing and secure moorings are available on an overnight basis. Pockets of industry cling on between Sneyd and Birchills but mostly the canal is accompanied by housing. A foundry near Wall End Bridge recently had five tons of aluminium stolen from it. Impudently, the thieves getaway vehicle was ... a narrowboat. Birchills Junction marks the egress of the W&E's Walsall Branch. The local power station, for many years the dominant feature of the branch

and source of considerable trade in coal boats, has been replaced by a retail park. Whether afoot or afloat, it's worth making the detour to the top of the Walsall flight at least. The generating plant brought considerable traffic to the canal. A sizeable unloading basin was serviced by overhead travelling cranes whose grabs lifted vast tonnages out of fleets of Joey boats.

The Walsall Branch terminated, prior to the construction of the Walsall Junction Canal and its flight of eight locks, at Birchills Wharf. Here, in 1900, a Boatmen's

continued overleaf:

continued overleaf:

Key *1*
1 site of power station
2 former Boatmen's Mission
3 former flour mill
4 site of Keays boatyard
5 site of copper works
6 site of Ryecroft mpd

*Figures relate to Wyrley & Essington - allow 2 hours for Walsall Canal

continued from page 79:

Mission or 'Rest' was built under the aegis of the Incorporated Seamen & Boatmen's Friendly Society. Its function was similar to that at Tipton (Map 8) but at Birchills an upper storey provided considerable dormitory facilities for day boatmen as well. Unfortunately, although the building had found appropriate use as a canal museum for a number of years, it closed due to shortfalls in local authority funding.

Walsall (Locks & Town Arm)

Walsall Locks were first mooted to link the Wyrley & Essington and Walsall canals in 1825, but the W&E and BCN companies were suspicious of each other's motives and proposal was followed by counter-proposal for fifteen years before the canal and its flight of eight locks, rising 65 feet, materialised. The flight - whose paddle gear is protected from vandalism by the need to employ water conservation keys - seems almost impervious to the landscape it occupies, as solitary predisposed as the men who invariably hover alongside it; with, or without dogs. The halfway point is overlooked by a lifesize crucifix of Christ, a war memorial attached to the end wall of St Andrews parish church. At street level there's a Madonna, adding weight to the suspicion that the church's congregation must belong to an especially devout Anglo-Catholic tradition; a piquant notion now in terraced streets palpably Muslim in atmosphere. Alongside Lock 7, fronting Wolverhampton Road, the old Albion flour mill has been converted into stylish apartments. An arched loading bay covers a side pond beside the lock chamber. Lock 6 is unique to the flight in having mitred bottom gates; the rest being more typical of BCN design with single leaves.

Walsall's Town Arm is in the process of being regenerated and already forms an off-beat gateway to the town's New Art Gallery, whose hundred foot high, terracotta-tiled tower provides a suitable climax. The boom, apparently, is there to keep flotsam and jetsam out of the basin, not boaters, and your bow should automatically push it aside. Anecdotal evidence, however, would have it that boat passages are rare, which is a shame, both for the canal and the town itself. We must all try harder! The Walsall Canal between Walsall and Great Bridge is described in the text accompanying Map 41.

Birchills - Little Bloxwich

Sunken wooden narrowboat hulls lie masked in reeds east of Birchills Junction, eloquent testimony to the BCN's busy past. There are no tangible remains, however, of the boat docks which once stood by Pratt's Mill Bridge - which, before being rebuilt in the 1930s, carried one of Walsall's tramway routes. Bowaters and Worseys - both famous Black Country boatbuilders - had premises here. In latter years the yard west of the bridge - now covered by housing - was operated by Peter Keay & Son, one of the last specialist wooden canal boat builders. Keays went into business after the Great War, based at first on the Daw End Branch, and were also known as canal carriers by virtue of their fleet of tugs which towed 'Joey' boats down from the Cannock coalfield. Joey was a BCN colloquialism for day boats without living accommodation used for short haul work. Tugs would pull 'trains' of these unpowered craft, or they might be worked singly by horses. They were equipped with transferable helms for bi-directional working, saving the need to turn in space-restricted basins.

An aqueduct carries the canal over the Walsall to Cannock railway. The original course of the canal was by-passed when the railway cutting was excavated, thus allowing the aqueduct to be built without disrupting canal trade. At Harden, Coal Pool and Little Bloxwich, housing borders the canal. Walsall's trolleybus service 15 used to weave its way through these estates until the system was lamentably abandoned in 1970. A half decent transport artist might do worse than replicate a close encounter at Coal Pool Bridge between a Brush-bodied Sunbeam and an Ernie Thomas tug on a train of Joeys bound for Birchills with Cannock coal.

Poverty stalked these post-war housing schemes and pilfering was commonplace when the coal boats passed by. Boat captains were apt to turn a blind eye, however flagrant the theft. The easiest approach was to board a boat at one bridge-hole, fill a bag with the black stuff, and alight at the next. Little Bloxwich is the last outpost of urbanisation. At Freeth's Bridge eastbound canal travellers wriggle free from the suffocation of the suburbs and escape into an open, level countryside which seems doubly beautiful in the light of what has gone before. Paradoxically, the working boatmen of the past would be passing from farmland into an area of collieries and iron works.

Wednesfield — Map 35

The big brick church of St Thomas - topped by a gold cockerel weathervane - lures you off the cut into Wednesfield's busy main street. Strange how these tangential Black Country communities contrive to stay so purposeful and relevant. This town's particular contribution to the industrial revolution was in the painful art of trap-making, though you must in turn not fall into the trap of underestimating its facilities, which are more ambitious than you'd think: banks (bless 'em), a street market on Tue, Fri & Sat, and some earthy Black Country retailers flying in the face of Sainsbury's by Rookery Bridge. Bentley Bridge retail park offers eating places (KFC, Pizza Hut, Nandos et al), a cinema complex, the opportunity to go ten-pin bowling, and visitor moorings alongside a new-build pub called The Nickelodeon. King Fryer fish & chips serendipitously placed by Church Bridge. Frequent buses to/from Wolverhampton and Walsall, not that the natives would ever dream of catching one.

Lane Head — Map 35

Dedicated visitor moorings and handy facilities make this a plausible semi-colon in your progress along the Curly Wyrley. Get a new tattoo, or put your mortgage on that 'dead cert' in the 4.10 at Fontwell.

Walsall — Map 36

Elevate the natural trajectory of your gaze and admire the town's rich architectural heritage, as exemplified by the Town Hall on Lichfield Street, whose foundation stone was laid by Prince Christian of Schleswig-Holstein - the Anglicised husband of Queen Victoria's third daugher, Helena and not, in the words of Palmerston, one of the three people who understood the thorny Schleswig-Holstein Question. Nearby is the bust of John Henry Carless, awarded a posthumous VC for 'most conspicuous bravery and devotion to

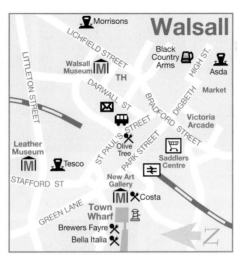

Walsall

duty' at the naval engagement of Heligoland Bight in 1917. All this and precious little space to elaborate on Sister Dora, Jerome K. Jerome, and sculptor, Jacob Epstein's muse and mistress, Kathleen Garman; all Walsallians by birth or adoption.

Eating & Drinking

BELLA ITALIA - Waterfront. Tel: 01922 897462. Italian cafe/restaurant open from 9am daily. WS2 8LR

BLACK COUNTRY ARMS - High Street. Tel: 01922 640588. Town pub of considerable character commended for food and beer alike. WS1 1QW

BREWERS FAYRE - Waterfront. Tel: 01922 651181. Breakfast from 6.30am (7 Sat & Sun). WS2 8LR

COSTA - Town Wharf. Tel: 01922 654400. Coffee shop with big glass window views over the basin. WS2 8LG

OLIVE TREE - St Pauls Street. Tel: 0794 157 0146. All day Greek restaurant opp. bus sta. WS1 1NR

ROSE & CROWN - Old Birchills. Tel: 01922 720533. Back street local serving Black Country Ales if you've worked up a thirst on the Walsall flight. WS2 8QH

Shopping

Walsall's thriving market dates from 1219 and attracts shoppers from all over the region. There are several busy precincts burgeoning with all the usual chain stores. Crown Wharf retail park abuts the canal terminus. The Victorian Arcade is all soaring glass, faded charm, and a fishmonger.

Things to Do

THE NEW ART GALLERY - Gallery Square. Open Tue-Sun admission free. Tel: 01922 654400. Lucky Walsall to have such a fine cultural facility. Surprisingly cosmopolitan range of exhibits by the likes of Cezanne, Van Gogh and Picasso. But we were especially taken with Stanislas Lepine's French landscape *The Canal*; discount the beam of the vessel depicted and it might have been the Wyrley & Essington. WS2 8LG

WALSALL LEATHER MUSEUM - Littleton Street. Tel: 01922 652288 Homage to the town's stock in trade; saddle making, lorinery, leather goods etc. Open Tue-Sat 10-5. WS2 8EN

WALSALL MUSEUM - Lichfield Street. Tel: 01922 653116. Small museum above the library with some interesting canal-related material. WS1 1TR

Connections

BUSES - alas no trolleybuses now - both the blue liveried vehicles of Walsall's fleet and the olive & primrose of Wolverhampton's are long gone, - but from the town's imposing modern bus station frequent services will take you to Wolverhampton, Wednesfield, Pelsall and Brownhills and other nodal points along the Wyrley & Essington Canal. Tel: 0871 200 2233.

TRAINS - local services to/from Rugeley (via Cannock), and Birmingham. Tel: 03457 484950.

B.C.N.
backwaters

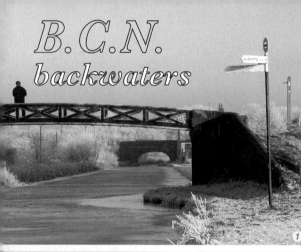

1 Pelsall Junction
2/3 Wednesfield
4 Darlaston
5 Tower Hill

JAMES BRIDGE AQUEDUCT

Anglesey Branch Canal

1 Walsall Locks
2 Ogley Junction
3 Boatmen's Mission
4 Norton Canes
5 Rushall Junction
6 Lane Head
7 Darlaston
8 Cannock Extension
9 Pelsall Junction

WYRLEY GROVE BRIDGE

WOLVERHAMPTON 13 MILES   CATSHILL JCN. 3¼ MILES

37 WYRLEY & ESSINGTON CANAL Brownhills 4mls/0lks/2hrs

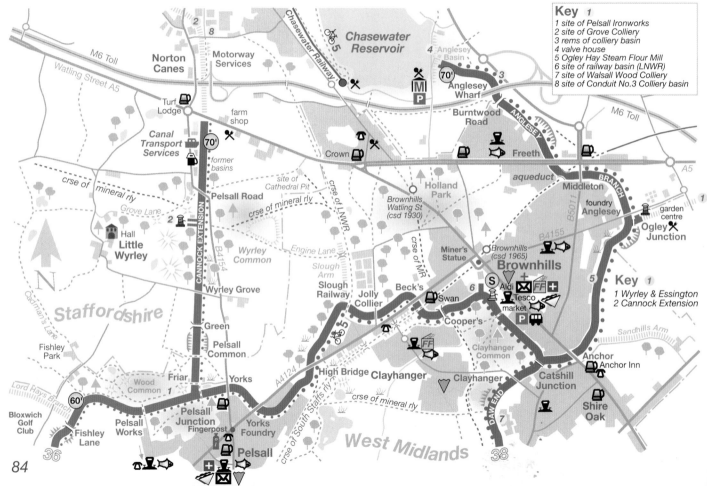

Key 1
1 site of Pelsall Ironworks
2 site of Grove Colliery
3 rems of colliery basin
4 valve house
5 Ogley Hay Steam Flour Mill
6 site of railway basin (LNWR)
7 site of Walsall Wood Colliery
8 site of Conduit No.3 Colliery basin

Key 1
1 Wyrley & Essington
2 Cannock Extension

Chasewater Reservoir

M6 Toll
Watling Street A5

Norton Canes
Motorway Services

Chasewater Railway

Anglesey Basin
Anglesey Wharf

M6 Toll
A5

Turf Lodge
farm shop

Canal Transport Services

Burntwood Road

ANGLESEY BRANCH

Crown
Freeth

Middleton
aqueduct

former basins

site of Cathedral Pit

Holland Park

foundry Anglesey

garden centre

Pelsall Road

crse of mineral rly

Grove Lane

CANNOCK EXTENSION

Brownhills Watling St (csd 1930)

crse of LNWR

Ogley Junction

B5011

B4155

Hall
Little Wyrley

Wyrley Common

Engine Lane

crse of MR

Miner's Statue

Brownhills (csd 1965)

Brownhills

Key 1
1 Wyrley & Essington
2 Cannock Extension

B4154

Wyrley Grove

Slough Arm

Slough Railway

Jolly Collier

Beck's

Aldi
Tesco market

FF

Green

Pelsall Common

Cooper's

Swan

Clayhanger Common

5

Anchor
Anchor Inn

N

Staffordshire

Fishley Park

Cadman's Lane

Friar

Pelsall Common

1

Yorks

High Bridge Clayhanger

A4124

Clayhanger

Catshill Junction

Sandhills Arm

Wood Common

DAW END

Shire Oak

Bloxwich Golf Club

Lord Hays Branch

60'

Fishley Lane

Pelsall Works

Pelsall Junction Fingerpost

Yorks Foundry

Pelsall

crse of South Staffs rly

crse of mineral rly

West Midlands

7

36

38

ONE might fill a book describing the histories and working practices of the canals, railways, iron works and collieries depicted on Map 37. This never less than fascinating section of the Wyrley & Essington Canal threw off seven arms or branches, three of which remain navigable. At Ogley Junction the W&E continued in an easterly direction, skirting Lichfield on its way to join the Coventry Canal at Huddlesford (Map 24). The Lichfield & Hatherton Canals Restoration Trust aims to restore this missing link as part of a revived route between the Staffordshire & Worcestershire Canal at Hatherton (Map 31) and Huddlesford. As for the arms and branches, the majority of them: Lord Hays Branch and the Gilpins, Slough and Sandhills arms, are long gone; but the Cannock Extension Canal (or at least a mile and a half of it), the Anglesey Branch and the Daw End Branch remain to tantalise the post-industrially predisposed.

Cannock Extension Canal

Sometimes known colloquially as the 'Top o' the Map', the Cannock Extension Canal opened in 1863 to tap the Cannock coalfield. It was five and three-quarter miles long, lockless, and terminated at Hednesford, a colliery town at the very foot of Cannock Chase. En route there was a junction at Church Bridge, where a precipitous flight of thirteen locks linked with the Hatherton Branch of the Staffs & Worcs Canal.

Paradoxically, mining subsidence brought about abandonment of the Cannock Extension above the A5 at Norton Canes at the end of 1962. Malcolm Braine's evocative account of a pleasure boat convoy's last cruise along the abandoned length appeared in the summer 2011 edition of *Narrow Boat* magazine.

The Extension was probably the last narrow gauge canal of any significant length to be built, and it has a distinctive character. Even in its decline, it retains a commercial sense of purpose. Blue 'Utopia' engineering bricks line its banks; BCN concrete fencing posts can be glimpsed in the undergrowth; and hefty, name-plated overbridges - more railway-like than canal - parenthesise its passage across the moody, back to nature landscape. White-clawed crayfish are reputed to reside beneath the surface.

Two old BCN cottages (No.s 211 & 212) adjoin the massive proportions of Friar Bridge. Opposite, old stables are in the process of being renovated as a dwelling. Wasteland extends westwards across Wood Common, a heathery, pock-marked site of a huge ironworks. Grove Colliery ceased production in 1952, though the basins continued to be employed as a loading point for boats until 1966 and remain used for moorings. In 1930, Grove pit was the scene of an underground explosion which killed fourteen miners. Ten of them are buried in a poignant row in the overflow of St James's churchyard, Brownhills. The miners' deaths might have attracted more coverage in the national press had the explosion not coincided with the crash of the airship R101 over northern France. Nearby, Little Wyrley Hall stands secluded behind high walls and security gates and barriers. Parts of its fabric can be traced back to Tudor times. British Railways Western Region Hall class locomotive 7913 bore its name.

Pelsall - Ogley

Pelsall Junction hosts boat rallies from time to time, but mostly few boats pass by, let alone negotiate the junction and head for Norton Canes. A shame, because this really is an evocative location to moor overnight, soaking up the haunted setting of post-industrial inactivity; all fir trees, loping foxes, and reedy ponds where once there were slag-heaps and mineral railways. Follow the footpath which leads to Fishley Park and you'll come upon a ruck of stones where John Wesley is said to have preached.

East of Pelsall the canal becomes an aquatic corset, keeping the housing estates at bay. Only occasionally does the whalebone burst as urbanisation spills across the cut. The Slough Arm was disused by the end of the 19th Century. It boasted two locks leading to a short summit fed by local springs and colliery pumping. One of what was a dense network of mineral railways rendered it obsolete. Its trackbed has become part of National Cycle Route No.5. Jolly Collier Bridge recalls the former existence of an inn offering stabling for canal horses. A rewatered arm extends into the former railway interchange basin at Brownhills, whilst a canoe centre provides boating facilities and visitor moorings. Pier Street footbridge provides access to Clayhanger Common, ninety acres of former mine workings redeveloped

continued overleaf:

continued from page 85

as a public open space. Long ago a canalside pub called The Fortunes of War stood here.

Catshill Junction is overlooked by a tower block and graced by an attractive sculpture, rather obscured now by vegetation. Both routes narrowed here to facilitate toll taking. The W&E proceeds from Catshill to Ogley passing the long vanished course of the Sandhills Arm, known to working boatmen as the 'Apple Arm' because it traversed an area of orchards. Farmland falls bucolically away to the east as the canal enters a shallow cutting of bracken and broom to reach Ogley Junction. East of Ogley, the Wyrley & Essington fell through a flight of locks which will have to be restored if the canal is to reconnect with the Coventry Canal at Huddlesford (Map 24). Encouragement has been given by the provision of an as yet unwatered aqueduct over the M6 Toll Road. Regrettably, much of the course of the W&E has been obliterated. Not far from here, the 'Staffordshire Hoard' of Saxon treasure was discovered by a metal-detecting enthusiast in 2009. Further items were found three years later.

Anglesey Branch

Chasewater Reservoir was opened in 1800 to supply the Wyrley & Essington main line with much needed water. Fifty years later, with the development of coal mining in the area, the feeder to Ogley was upgraded to navigable standards. Nowadays the branch represents the furthest north you can travel on the BCN.

There are views north-east beyond the M6 Toll road of the three spires of Lichfield Cathedral. An aqueduct carries the canal over the trackbed of the South Staffordshire Railway, before you pass beneath the A5 - alias Watling Street - and the M6 Toll to reach Anglesey Basin, an expanse of water as remote as anything the inland waterways system has to offer. The last consignments of coal were loaded here in the late Sixties and solely some contorted lumps of metal recall the existence of the wharf's complex loading apparatus. Chasewater Reservoir lies enigmatically beyond its elevated rim. In 2010, when it was dewatered for maintenance to be undertaken, two Second World War bombs were exposed on its bed.

Pelsall   Map 37

The centre, with facilities aplenty, is grouped around a pleasant green, a mile to the south of the canal. In St Michael's churchyard stands a memorial to the victims of the Pelsall Hall Colliery Disaster of 1872.

Eating & Drinking

THE FINGER POST - Yorks Bridge. Tel: 01922 693707. Canalside pub formerly known as the Royal Oak. Bar and restaurant food. WS3 5AU

Brownhills   Map 37

Brownhills' forty feet high miner's statue towers over the town like a Soviet Bloc sculpture of Stalinist proportions, reminding us all (very necessarily now) why the town was built here in the first place. The long main street exemplifies its era, the lacklustre shop frontages harbouring no ambitions above the monotony of two storeys, save at Catshill where monolithic high rise flats also echo Eastern Europe.

Eating & Drinking

THE ANCHOR - Chester Road (by Anchor Bridge near Catshill Junction). Tel: 01543 360219. Modern Marston's pub, food and Sky Sports. WS8 6DP.
MARIO'S FISH BAR & RESTAURANT - High Street. Tel: 01543 371487. Eat in or take-away. WS8 6HL
SWAN - Pelsall Road (accessible off towpath between Beck's and Jolly Collier bridges). Tel: 01543 820628. *Good Beer Guide* listed local serving Holdens and guests. WS8 7DL

Shopping

On Tuesdays and Saturdays the canalside market throbs with activity. There are Tesco and Aldi supermarkets adjacent to the canal's Silver Street visitor moorings.

Things to Do

CHASEWATER RAILWAY - Tel: 01543 452623. Trains operate on Sundays most of the year and additionally on selected days in summer along two miles of old mineral lines. Museum/cafe/souvenir shop. WS8 7NL

FOREST OF MERCIA INNOVATION CENTRE - Chasewater. Tel: 01543 308860. HQ of Community Forest. Refreshments and souvenirs. WS8 7NL The Beowulf Brewing Co's premises occupy one of the neighbouring industrial units. Their bottle-conditioned beers are available (in minimum packs of a dozen) direct from the plant. Tel: 01543 454067. WS8 7NL.

Connections

Both Brownhills' railway stations having closed, buses offer the only means of public transport. Frequent links with Walsall, Aldridge and Rushall are a boon for towpath explorers. Tel: 0871 200 2233.

Rushall   Map 38

An Indian restaurant (Royal Oak - Tel: 01922 614947) and two pubs (Boat House and Manor Arms) provide canalside refreshment opportunities at Daw End Bridge. Just west of the canal is a Chinese takeaway - Tel: 01922 624255. Half a mile further down the B4154 are convenience stores, fish & chips and a McDonald's.

THE navvies who laboured to build the Daw End Branch of the Wyrley & Essington Canal probably wouldn't recognise it now. When it opened in 1800, as a link to the limestone quarries at Hay Head, it was a typical contour canal, crossing a district largely innocent of industry and urbanisation. But it soon became apparent that the hinterland of Brownhills was rich in clay deposits, and brick and tile making became the staple activities of the area. Coal mining prospered too, bequeathing a legacy of subsidence which wrought havoc with the canal bed, necessitating continual heightening of its banks, so that it came to resemble a Fenland river. So it's likely that old-stagers would furrow their brows in amazement to see their cut twisting and turning high above the rest of the crumbling landscape, whilst today's canal travellers find themselves somewhat voyeuristically at bedroom and bathroom level of houses lining the canal at Walsall Wood: some of those wallpapers are hard to take seriously.

truly long distance narrowboat cargo of note.

On a winter Saturday afternoon, you could do worse than moor up at Daw End Bridge and go and watch Rushall Olympic FC battling it out in the Evo-Stick League against the illustrious likes of Blyth Spartans, Nantwich Town and Frickley Athletic. 'The Pics' can trace their roots back to the 19th Century when miners from Aldridge Colliery formed an ad hoc side. Delightfully, in match reports, they are apt to refer to their No.1, not as a mere goalkeeper, but as a 'custodian'. Truly the olympic ideal lives on in this corner of the Black Country.

At Longwood the Daw End Branch turned eastwards to reach the limestone workings at Hay Head, and there was no canal link southwards until the merger of the BCN and W&E in 1840. The Rushall Canal was an offspring of this union though, maintaining the connubial metaphor, there is reason to believe that the resultant waterway was by way of being an accident of careless family planning. Apparently the BCN began to have doubts about the viability of the proposed link, only to be reminded that Government money borrowed under the Act of Union with the W&E would have to be returned should the Rushall Canal not be built!

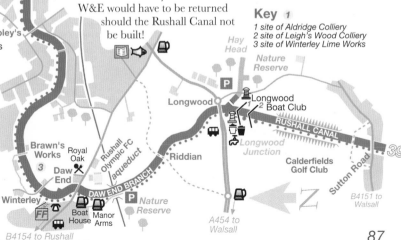

Key 1

1 site of Aldridge Colliery
2 site of Leigh's Wood Colliery
3 site of Winterley Lime Works

Walsall Wood was the location of 'The Traveller', probably the last pub in England to offer stabling for canal horses. The Utopia blue bricks we discovered on the Cannock Extension were apparently made in a canalside works near Northwood Bridge. These days the local industry seems more concerned with burying refuse in seagull-haunted clay pits. More memories are evoked at Hopley's Bridge where Duckham's canalside works was the recipient of the ill-fated Birmingham & Midland oil consignments from Ellesmere Port in 1970; perhaps the last

BLACK Country seagulls cry nasally over the Tame Valley Canal, being perhaps the transmuted spirits of former boatmen. Yet even the most committed BCN die-hard would admit that the canals featured on this map hardly represent the system at its most scintillating. Suffocated by suburbia and motorways, unrelievedly straight - and therefore lacking the inherent 'mystery' of the classic winding canal - they don't have the dynamism of the industrialised BCN at its best. Such criticisms, though, are relative, and it would be an unimaginative canal explorer who fails to find something, at least, of interest in the characters of these two routes. Rushall Locks were nicknamed 'The Ganzies' by working boatmen, reputedly because of the thick Guernsey style sweaters favoured by steerers on this windswept cut. In the pound between locks 6 and 7 stood Bell Wharf, one of the few predominantly agricultural basins to be found on the BCN.

Half on embankments, half in cuttings, the Tame Valley Canal's most dramatic incident is its crossing, on an imposing three-arch aqueduct, of the Grand Junction Railway; a rare case (possibly unique - suggestions otherwise gratefully received) of a railway pre-dating an adjoining canal. We were intrigued by the proliferation - west of Stone Cross - of side bridges. Our trusty 1904 6" Ordnance map showed them to have spanned arms serving sandpits and small collieries. Holloway Bank Bridge carries Telford's Holyhead Turnpike road across the canal at Hill Top. Apparently the road here was so steep that passengers had to climb the hill on foot whilst the horses strained to haul their carriages up unloaded. The region's Metro system also crosses the canal here, its brightly painted modern trams emphasising the archaic nature of passing boats.

The Tame Valley Canal is equipped with towpaths on both of its banks. Generally speaking west of Rushall Junction this is better on the north side, whilst south of Rushall it's better to the west.

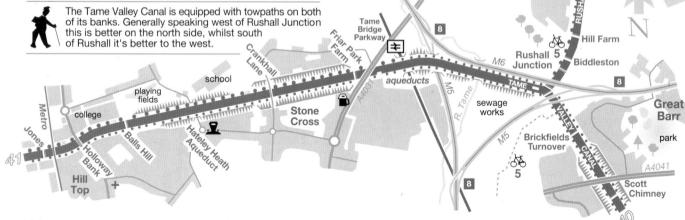

40 TAME VALLEY CANAL Hamstead & Perry Barr 4mls/13lks/3hrs

ONCE upon a time, before the navvies dug this latecomer, the Tame must have been a pretty enough watercourse, skipping gaily down off the Black Country ridge to its confluence with the Trent above Tamworth. Not that the canal can be blamed for the urbanisation of the valley. Save for Hamstead Colliery (whose basin by Gorse Farm Bridge was linked by tramway to the pit head) the Tame Valley Canal attracted little industry to its banks hereabouts, being built primarily - and remaining useful throughout its commercial life - as a by-pass route, enabling through traffics to avoid the centre of Birmingham. No, these fields were filled by the phenomenon of the housing estate which, from the late nineteen-thirties onwards, crept northwards from burgeoning Birmingham, creating subtopias out of Perry Barr, Witton and Hamstead. Fortunately, all these Englishmen's castles fail to smother the canal which, either hides in rocky, wooded cuttings reminiscent of 'The Shroppie', or rides upon embankments with views southwards over the Second City. From here it doesn't look far - but it's the best part of a day's boating away!

Two aqueducts of differing design carry the canal above the rooftops of Hamstead. You may care to scramble down the embankment to view them from a different perspective. The local colliery closed in the early Sixties. In 1908 there was an underground fire at the pit which claimed the lives of twenty-five miners. One of the trapped groups, anticipating their doom, chalked their names on a nearby door together with the poignant inscription: "The Lord preserve us for we are all trusting in Christ." Rescue teams with special breathing apparatus were sent from the Yorkshire coalfield, and one of these men, John Welsby, lost his own life, heroically searching for the trapped men. He is commemorated by a street named after him on the estate which covers the site of the mine.

Locally known as Walsall Road, the A34 encounters its fair share of canals on its journey from Southampton to Manchester - ten at a rough count - though these old trunk roads have fallen into obscurity in the motorway era. Perry Barr Locks - colloquially known as the 'New Thirteen' (as opposed to the 'Old Thirteen' at Farmers Bridge (Map 20) - lie adjacent to Perry Park with its impressive athletics stadium. The chambers are fitted with double bottom gates throughout. A good old-fashioned lock-keeper resides at the top of the flight where boating facilities (including showers) are laid on, though one suspects, rarely used. By the time the foot of the flight has been reached, the canal finds itself re-entering Birmingham's industrial zone. Travelling southbound, the suburban dream is over.

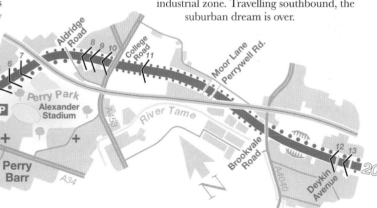

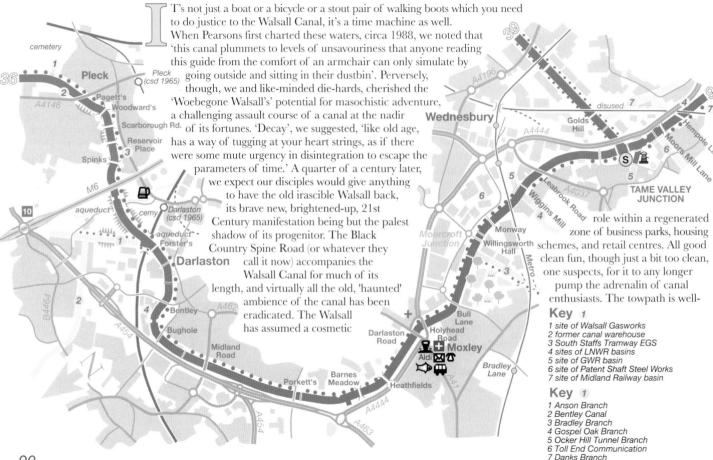

IT's not just a boat or a bicycle or a stout pair of walking boots which you need to do justice to the Walsall Canal, it's a time machine as well. When Pearsons first charted these waters, circa 1988, we noted that 'this canal plummets to levels of unsavouriness that anyone reading this guide from the comfort of an armchair can only simulate by going outside and sitting in their dustbin'. Perversely, though, we and like-minded die-hards, cherished the 'Woebegone Walsall's' potential for masochistic adventure, a challenging assault course of a canal at the nadir of its fortunes. 'Decay', we suggested, 'like old age, has a way of tugging at your heart strings, as if there were some mute urgency in disintegration to escape the parameters of time.' A quarter of a century later, we expect our disciples would give anything to have the old irascible Walsall back, its brave new, brightened-up, 21st Century manifestation being but the palest shadow of its progenitor. The Black Country Spine Road (or whatever they call it now) accompanies the Walsall Canal for much of its length, and virtually all the old, 'haunted' ambience of the canal has been eradicated. The Walsall has assumed a cosmetic role within a regenerated zone of business parks, housing schemes, and retail centres. All good clean fun, though just a bit too clean, one suspects, for it to any longer pump the adrenalin of canal enthusiasts. The towpath is well-

Key 1
1 site of Walsall Gasworks
2 former canal warehouse
3 South Staffs Tramway EGS
4 sites of LNWR basins
5 site of GWR basin
6 site of Patent Shaft Steel Works
7 site of Midland Railway basin

Key 1
1 Anson Branch
2 Bentley Canal
3 Bradley Branch
4 Gospel Oak Branch
5 Ocker Hill Tunnel Branch
6 Toll End Communication
7 Danks Branch

surfaced, and its banks are becoming overlooked by neat houses, and the threat of hooliganism recedes. But - and it's a 'Big Woolwich Butty' of a but - what dyed-in-the-wool canal enthusiast, head full of fantasies of carrying coke to Coseley and timber to Tipton, is going to derive any gratification from walking or boating along a concrete-banked waterway threading its way through housing estates and retail parks and accompanied by a dual-carriageway? Friends, Romans and Blackcountrymen, we've come to bury the Walsall Canal, not necessarily to praise it.

Bearing generally southwards from Walsall - generally, that is, in the context of a contour canal - the Walsall runs through the suburb of Pleck. Walsall gasworks, was a relatively late user of canal transport: coal in and waste products out. Thomas Clayton's very last run was from here with crude tar to Oldbury on 31st March, 1966 aboard the motor boat *Stour* now resident at the BCLM. A former warehouse catches the eye on the opposite bank, and a substantial mosque breaths fresh life into an otherwise predominently debauched scene. When we last passed a pint of mild at Pleck Workingmen's Club would put you back a mere £1.50.

The canal slips through a sandy cutting and then passes the levelled site of James Bridge copper works. Nip up the steps at Reservoir Place Bridge, turn right, and you'll come upon the once proud premises of the South Staffordshire Tramways Electric Generating Station, erected in 1892. Coal was brought in by canal boat to feed the furnaces.

Emerging from beneath the M6 motorway, the canal rides upon a considerable embankment carrying it over a by-road and the infant River Tame. On one side of the embankment stands a casino, on the other a cemetery: the long and short odds of life in eloquent juxtaposition. Bullrushes thrive at the entrance to the Anson Branch which connected with the Bentley Canal, abandoned in 1961 (see also Map 35).

Crossing the Grand Junction Railway, the canal essays a loop around the old metal-bashing town of Darlaston. By Bughole Bridge the Spine Road makes itself known to southbound canal travellers for the first time - you are not encouraged to become bosom pals. Pipes, pylons and Poundland's gargantuan warehouse are poor substitutes for the rip-roaring past, and you find yourself wondering who exactly Mr Porkett was, and what would he think of the vacuous present.

Telford's Holyhead Road crosses the canal at Moxley. Redevelopment has eroded much of the latent atmosphere of the canal as it reaches Moorcroft Junction. Until its closure in 1961, the Bradley Branch led off from here to the Wednesbury Oak Loop, ascending to the Wolverhampton Level through a flight of nine locks. A footpath follows the course of this interesting route, past abandoned lock chambers, to a public open space circling housing estates.

Of the once vast Patent Shaft Steel Works there is no trace, neither does the Gospel Oak Branch lead anymore to Willingsworth furnaces. Opposite its reedy remains - shot like a green arrow into the entrails of a housing estate - a side bridge spans the entrance to the Great Western Railway's Wednesbury rail/canal interchange basin. Sleek as they are, the Metro's trams are a poor substitute for the King-hauled, Paddington expresses of yesteryear.

The contemporary face of transport, in the shape of huge lorry-served warehouses, mocks the emasculated canal as it reaches Tame Valley Junction, where boating facilities (including showers and self-operated pump-out) are laid on. Limited secure visitor moorings are also available. The Tame Valley Canal egresses dolefully eastwards, offering alternative routes to Brownhills and Birmingham. To the south another through route has been lost. The Tipton Green & Toll End Communication Canal doesn't exactly roll off the tongue, but until 1960 it 'communicated' with the main line at Tipton, easing congestion in the heyday of the BCN when boats were apt to be choc-a-bloc at Ryders Green.

Alan Godfrey's reprint of the 1902 Ordnance Survey Map for Great Bridge & Toll End depicts in all its fascinating complexity the stretch of canal between Toll End Junction and Ryders Green Bottom Lock. Here the Danks Branch made its dog-leg connection with the Tame Valley Canal, whilst the South Staffordshire Railway spanned the Walsall's main line. It still does (though its tracks haven't seen a train in years - and await the clarion call to become part of the Metro system, linking Walsall with Dudley) but virtually all trace of the extensive London & North Western rail/canal interchange basins have vanished into a swampy undergrowth abutting the Spine Road. Hempole Lane Bridge is date-stamped 1825 in Roman numerals - strap us into our time machines ...

This Guide

Pearson's Canal Companions are a long established, independently produced series of guide books devoted to the inland waterways and designed to appeal equally to boaters, walkers, cyclists and other, not readily pigeon-holed - though no less deserving - members of society. Considerable pride is taken to make these guides as up to date, accurate, entertaining and inspirational as possible. A good guide book should fulfil three functions: make you want to go; interpret the lie of the land when you're there; and provide a lasting souvenir of your journeys.

The Maps

There are forty-one numbered maps whose layout is shown by the Route Planner inside the front cover. Maps 1-19 show the route of the Stourport Ring; and Maps 7-10 and 20-32 the route of the Black Country Ring. Maps 33/34 cover the Stourbridge and Dudley Canals, whilst Maps 35-41 cover the northern area of the Birmingham Canal Navigations.

The maps - measured imperially like the waterways they depict, and not being slavishly north-facing - are easily read in either direction. Users will thus find most itineraries progressing smoothly and logically from left to right or vice versa. Figures quoted at the top of each map refer to distance per map, locks per map and average cruising time. An alternative indication of timings from centre to centre can be found on the Route Planner.

Obviously, cruising times vary with the nature of your boat and the number of crew at your disposal, so quoted times should be taken only as an estimate. Neither do times quoted take into account any delays which might occur at lock flights in high season. Walking and cycling times - not indicated on the maps - will depend very much on the state of individual sections of towpath and the stamina of those concerned.

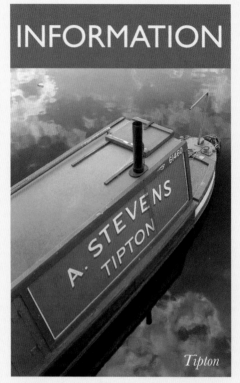

INFORMATION

Tipton

The Text

Each map is accompanied by a route commentary placing the waterway in its historic, social and topographical context. As close to each map as is feasible, gazetteer-like entries are given for places passed through, listing, where appropriate, facilities of likely benefit to users of this guide.

Walking

The simplest way to go canal exploring is on foot along the towpaths originally provided so that horses could 'tow' boats. Walking costs largely nothing and you are free to concentrate on the passing scene; something that boaters, with the responsibilities of navigation thrust upon them, are not always at liberty to do. The maps set out to give some idea of the quality of the towpath on any given section of canal. More of an art than a science to be sure, but at least it reflects our personal experiences, and whilst it does vary from area to area, none of it should prove problematical for anyone inured to the vicissitudes of country walking. We recommend the use of public transport to facilitate 'one-way' itineraries but stress the advisability of checking up to date details on the telephone numbers quoted, or on the websites of National Rail Enquiries or Traveline for trains and buses respectively.

Cycling

Bicycling along towpaths is an increasingly popular pastime, though one not always equally popular with other waterway users such as boaters, anglers and pedestrians. It is important to remember that you are sharing the towpath with other people out for their own form of enjoyment, and to treat them with the respect and politeness they deserve. A bell is a useful form of diplomacy; failing that, a stentorian cough. Happily, since the inception of the Canal & River Trust in 2012, it is no longer necessary for cyclists to acquire a permit to use the towpath.

Boating

Boating on inland waterways is an established, though relatively small, facet of the UK tourist industry. It is also, increasingly, a chosen lifestyle. There are approximately 30,000 privately owned boats registered on the canals, but in addition to these, numerous firms offer boats for hire. These range from small operators with half a dozen boats to sizeable fleets run by companies with several bases.

Most hire craft have all the creature comforts you are likely to expect. In the excitement of planning a boating holiday you may give scant thought to the contents of your hire boat, but at the end of a hard day's boating such matters take on more significance, and a well equipped, comfortable boat, large enough to accommodate your crew with something to spare, can make the difference between a good holiday and one which will be shudderingly remembered for the wrong reasons.

Traditionally, hire boats are booked out by the week or fortnight, though many firms now offer more flexible short breaks or extended weeks. All reputable hire firms give newcomers tuition in boat handling and lock working, and first-timers soon find themselves adapting to the pace of things 'on the cut'.

Navigational Advice

Newcomers, hiring a boat on the inland waterways for the first time, have every right to expect sympathetic and thorough tuition from the company providing their boat. Boat-owners are, by definition, likely to be already adept at navigating. The following, however, may prove useful points of reference.

Locks are part of the charm of canal cruising, but they are potentially dangerous environments for children, pets and careless adults. Use of them should be methodical and unhurried, whilst special care should be exercised in rain, frost and snow when slippery hazards abound.

Apart from the basin locks at Diglis, Worcester and the automated locks on the River Severn between Worcester and Stourport, all the locks on the canals covered by this guide are of the familiar narrow-beam variety. All gates should be closed on leaving each

Aldersley Junction

chamber (unless courteously leaving them open for an approaching boat) and all paddles wound down. A high proportion of locks in urban areas are fitted with security gear to combat hooliganism, and boaters should ensure that they are equipped with 'handcuff' (aka 'T' or water conservation) keys to release the paddle gear. These are obtainable by post from CART or from boatyards.

The River Severn locks at Bevere, Holt and Lincomb are mechanised and manned. It's not a bad idea to telephone ahead when joining the river at Worcester or Stourport to Bevere or Lincomb locks respectively to let them know you are on the way if you're not intending to stop en route. Once you've negotiated one lock the grapevine tends to alert the keepers to your progress. Be guided by the colour light signals, but wait for the signal to turn green and the gates to open before approaching too closely. The chambers of these locks are large and you may be sharing with other craft. Steadying straps and chains are attached to the chamber walls and these can be hand held to control your boat if there is any turbulence. Always follow the lock-keeper's advice. He will be in his control cabin as you pass through the lock.

The basin locks at Worcester and Stourport are only open during timetabled hours - as indeed are the river locks mentioned above. Hire craft are likely to have up to date timings in their boat manuals, but private boaters can obtain details from the Canal & River Trust.

Finally, it behoves us all to be on our best behaviour at locks. Remember to exercise a little 'give and take'. The use of fists to decide precedence at locks is one canal tradition not worthy of preservation.

Floods can occur on the River Severn at any time of year at short notice. Officials should be on hand to help and advise at such times. If you are already on the river you must tie up at the nearest official moorings and remain there until further notice. At times of flood you may be denied access to the river. Boat hire companies are familiar with the Severn's moods and will be sympathetic to genuine delays.

Mooring on the canals featured in this guide is per usual practice - ie on the towpath side, away from sharp bends, bridge-holes and narrows. A 'yellow' bollard symbol represents visitor mooring sites; either as designated officially or, in some cases as recommended by our personal experience. Of course, one of the great joys of canal boating has always been the ability to moor wherever (sensibly) you like. In recent years, however, it has become obvious, particularly in urban areas, that there are an increasing number of undesirable locations where mooring is not to be recommended for fear of vandalism, theft or abuse. It would be nice if local authorities would see their way to providing pleasant, secure, overnight facilities for passing boaters who, after all, bring the commerce of tourism in their wake. Few boaters would object to making a small payment, as is the custom on a number of river navigations.

Moveable Bridges are an occasional feature of the canals. Some 'swing', some 'lift', some are manually or windlass-operated, some mechanised. Some require either a CART 'facilities' Yale key and/or 'handcuff' key to facilitate their moving. Always return them to the position you found them in after use unless it is obvious that another boat is approaching to use them.

Tunnels occur at a number of points on the canals included in this guide and are great fun to negotiate. Pets and young children should be kept 'indoors'. Steerers are advised to wear waterproofs!

Turning points on the canals are known as 'winding holes'; pronounced as the thing which blows because in the old days the wind was expected to do much of the work rather than the boatman. Winding holes capable of taking a full length boat of around seventy foot length are marked where appropriate on the maps. Winding holes capable of turning shorter craft are marked with the approximate length. It is of course also possible to turn boats at junctions and at most boatyards, though in the case of the latter it is considered polite to ask permission before doing so.

'Bull & Bladder'

Boating facilities are provided at regular intervals along the inland waterways, and range from a simple water tap or refuse disposal skip, to the provision of sewage disposal, showers and laundry. Such vital features are also obtainable at boatyards and marinas along with repairs and servicing. An alphabetical list of boatyards appears on page 95.

Dimension restrictions vary from waterway to waterway. Up to date details can be obtained from the Canal & River Trust.

Closures (or 'stoppages' in the arcane parlance of the canals) traditionally occur on the inland waterways between November and April, during which time most of the heavy maintenance work is undertaken. Occasionally, however, an emergency stoppage, or perhaps water restriction, may be imposed at short notice, closing part of the route you intend to use. Up to date details are posted at key locations throughout the inland waterways network. They are also available from CART online or from hire bases.

Canal & River Trust

CART are the body responsible for the canals and rivers in this guide. Their head office address is:
First Floor North, Station House,
500 Elder Gate, Milton Keynes, MK9 1BB
Tel: 0303 040 4040
www.canalrivertrust.org.uk

Societies

The Inland Waterways Association was founded in 1946 to campaign for retention of the canal system. Many routes now open to pleasure boaters may not have been so but for this organisation. Membership details, together with details of the IWA's regional branches, may be obtained from: Inland Waterways Association, Island House, Moor Road, Chesham HP5 1WA. Tel: 01494 783453. *www.waterways.org.uk*
A number of the canals featured in this guide are also supported by individual societies:
BCN Society - *www.bcnsociety.co.uk*
Lapal Canal Trust - *www.lapal.org*
Lichfield & Hatherton Canals Restoration Trust - *www.lhcrt.org.uk*
Staffordshire & Worcestershire Canal Society - *www.swcanalsociety.co.uk*
Stourbridge Navigation Trust - *www.thebondedwarehousestourbridge.co.uk*
Trent & Mersey Canal Society - *www.trentandmerseycanalsociety.co.uk*
Worcester-Birmingham & Droitwich Canals Society *www.wbdcs.org.uk*

Acknowledgements

Thanks to Meg Gregory for the sign-written cover; to Mark Smith and Andy Cope; to Karen Tanguy who facilitated the author's research trips and generally ensured the book's smooth passage to the printers; and to those selfsame printers, Hawksworth of Uttoxeter.

BOATING DIRECTORY

Hire Bases

ABC BOAT HIRE - Worcester & Birmingham Canal Maps 13 & 17; Staffs & Worcs Canal Map 31. PO Box 232, Worcester WR1 2SD. Tel: 0330 333 0590 www.abcboathire.com

ANGLO WELSH WATERWAY HOLIDAYS - Worcs & Birmingham Canal Map 14 and Staffs & Worcs Canal Map 28. 2 The Hide Market, West Street, Bristol BS2 0BH. Tel: 0117 304 1122 www.anglowelsh.co.uk

BLACK PRINCE HOLIDAYS - Worcester & Birmingham Canal Map 14. Stoke Prior, Bromsgrove, Worcestershire B60 4LA. Tel: 01527 575115 www.black-prince.com

BROOK LINE - Worcester & Birmingham Canal Map 16. Dunhampstead Wharf, Oddingley, Droitwich, Worcs. WR9 7JX. Tel: 01905 773889. www.brookline.co.uk

DRAYTON NARROW BOAT HIRE - Birmingham & Fazeley Canal Map 23. Coleshill Road, Fazeley, Tamworth, Staffs. B78 3RY Tel: 01827 262042 www.drayton-narrowboat-holidays.co.uk

MARINE CRUISES - Kings Bromley Wharf, Trent & Mersey Canal Map 25. Lichfield Road, Bromley Hayes, Staffs. Tel: 01244 373911 WS13 8HT www.marinecruises.co.uk

NAPTON NARROWBOATS - Staffs & Worcs Canal Map 7. Oxley Moor Road, Wolverhampton WV9 5HW. Tel: 01902 789942 www.napton-marina.co.uk

STARLINE NARROWBOATS - Staffs & Worcs Canal Map 1. Engine Lane, Stourport-on-Severn, Worcs DY13 9EP. Tel: 01531 632003. www.starlinenarrowboats.co.uk

Boatyards

ALVECHURCH MARINA - Alvechurch, Worcester & Birmingham Canal, Map 13. Tel: 0121 445 1133. B48 7SQ

ANGLO WELSH - Gt. Haywood, Staffs & Worcs Canal, Map 28. Tel: 01889 881711. ST18 0RJ

ANGLO WELSH - Tardebigge, Worcester & Birmingham Canal, Map 14. Tel: 01527 873898. B60 1LR

ASHWOOD MARINA - Ashwood, Staffs & Worcs Canal, Map 4. Tel: 01384 295535. DY6 0AQ.

BLACK PRINCE - Stoke Prior, Worcester & Birmingham Canal, Map 14. Tel: 01527 575115. B60 4LA

BROOK LINE - Oddingley, Worcester & Birmingham Canal Map 16. Tel: 01905 773889. WR9 7JX

CAGGY'S - Tipton, BCN Map 8. Tel: 0121 520 5362. DY4 8EZ

CANAL TRANSPORT SERVICES - Cannock Extension Canal Map 37. Tel: 01543 374370. WS3 5AP

COOMBESWOOD CANAL TRUST - Hawne Basin, Dudley No.2 Canal, Map 34. Tel: 0121 550 1355. B62 8AW

CRAFTED BOATS - Stoke Prior, Worcs & B'ham Canal, Map 14. Tel: 01527 876438. B60 4JZ

DIGLIS BASIN MARINA - Worcester & Birmingham Canal, Map 17. Tel: 01905 356314. WR5 3BW

FAZELEY MILL MARINA - Birmingham & Fazeley Canal Map 23. Tel: 01827 261138. B78 3SE

JD BOAT SERVICES - Staffs & Worcs Canal Map 31. Tel: 01902 791811. ST19 5PR

KINGS BROMLEY MARINA - Trent & Mersey Canal Map 25. Tel: 01543 417209. WS13 8HT

KINGS ORCHARD MARINA - Coventry Canal Map 25. Tel: 01543 433608. WS13 8SP

LIMEKILN CHANDLERS - Stourport, Staffs & Worcs Canal Map 1. Tel: 01299 821111. DY13 9EL

MARINE SERVICES FRADLEY - Fradley, Coventry/Trent & Mersey Canals Map 25. Tel: 01283 790332. DE13 7DN

NAPTON NARROWBOATS - Autherley, Staffs & Worcs Map 6/7. Tel: 01902 789942. WV9 5HW.

OXLEY MARINE - Autherley, Staffs & Worcs Canal Map 6/7. Tel: 01902 789522. WV10 6TZ

OTHERTON BOAT HAVEN - Penkridge, Staffs & Worcs Canal Map 30. Tel: 01785 712515. ST19 5NX

SHERBORNE WHARF - Birmingham, BCN, Map 11. Tel: 0121 455 6163. B16 8DE

STREETHAY WHARF - Lichfield, Coventry Canal Map 25. Tel: 01543 414808. WS13 8RJ

TEDDESLEY BOAT CO - Staffs & Worcs Canal Map 30. Tel: 01785 714692. ST19 5RH

WORCESTER MARINA - Worcester & Birmingham Canal, Map 17. Tel: 01905 734160. WR1 2RS

Day Boat Hire

ABC BOAT HIRE - Alvechurch, Worcester & Birmingham, Map 13. Tel: 0121 445 1133. B48 7SQ

ANGLO WELSH - Tardebigge, Worcester & Birmingham, Map 14. B60 1LR Gt Haywood, Staffs & Worcs, Map 28. Tel: 0117 304 1122. ST18 0RJ

PITCHCROFT BOAT STATION - River Severn, Worcester, Map 17. Tel: 01905 27949. WR1 3EZ

STREETHAY WHARF - Coventry Canal, Map 25. Tel: 01543 414808. WS13 8RJ

Nine More Reasons for Exploring the Canals with Pearsons

9th edition - ISBN 978 0 9562777 4 9

10th edition - ISBN 978 0 9562777 8 7

9th edition - ISBN 978 0 9562777 7 0

1st edition - ISBN 978 0 9928492 1 4

7th edition - ISBN 978 0 9562777 5 6

9th edition - ISBN 978 0 9562777 3 2

8th edition - ISBN 978 0 9562777 9 4

1st edition - ISBN 978 0 9928492 0 7

3rd edition - ISBN 978 0 9562777 6 3

Pearson's Canal Companions are published by Wayzgoose. They are widely available from hire bases, boatyards, canal shops, good bookshops, via Amazon and other internet outlets.